The Farm on the Hill
He Calls Home

The Farm on the Hill
He Calls Home

John B. Lee

Black Moss Press
Settlements Series
2004

© Copyright John B. Lee 2004

National Library of Canada Cataloguing in Publication

Lee, John B., 1951-
    The farm on the hill we call home / by John B. Lee.

(Settlement series ; 1)
ISBN 0-88753-394-9

    1. Lee, John B., 1951- —Childhood and youth. 2. Farm life—Ontario, Southwestern. 3. Poets, Canadian (English)—Biography. I. Title. II. Series: Settlement series (Windsor, Ont.) ; 1.

PS8573.E348Z466 2004   C811'.54   C2004-901871-X

Published by Black Moss Press at 2450 Byng Road, Windsor, Ontario N8W 3E8.

This is the first in a series called SETTLEMENTS, a series that focuses upon neighbourhoods and regions in Canada.

The author wishes to thank Patricia Black, Sheila Martindale, and Roger Bell for their assistance in the copy editing of the text and Marty Gervais for suggesting that he write it.

Parts of *The Farm on the Hill He Calls Home* have appeared in *Head Heart Hands Health: a History of 4H in Ontario; The Ridgetown Independent; Windsor Review;* and *Tower Poetry Society web site*

Black Moss books are distributed by Firefly Books, 66 Leek Crescent, Richmond Hill, ON Canada L4B 1H1. U.S. orders should be directed to Firefly Books at 4 Daybreak Lane, Westport, CT U.S.A. 06880-2157.

Black Moss gratefully acknowledges the generous support given by the Canada Council for the Arts and the Ontario Arts Council for its publishing program.

Le Conseil des Arts | The Canada Council
du Canada | for the Arts

ONTARIO ARTS COUNCIL
CONSEIL DES ARTS DE L'ONTARIO

for my father, George Emerick Lee

September 22, 1922-March 19, 2004

"...the path to a successful literary career begins with reading and ends without farming..."

Raymond Knister

table of contents

preface

I'VE HOED BEANS. Mowed hay. Painted barns. Slopped hogs. Thrashed wheat. Built houses. Broken cattle. Shovelled corn. Mucked pens. Dug graves. Stooked grain. Slaughtered hogs. Driven truck. Ploughed land. Burned stubble. Worked fields. Cut boars. Shorn sheep. Bulled cows. Fixed fences. Watered livestock. Shown heifers. Polished halters. Blown stumps. Pitched straw. Culled runts. Trimmed horns. Wrung bulls. Castrated cattle. I've inoculated the sick and helped with the midnight calving hot to the shoulder in breech. I've done all that and more. And that was before I was ten years old.

I've worked hard and slept keen.

As a boy growing up on a farm, I knew what it was to feel dog tired and yet to work on into the gloaming of summer and then to sleep the sleep of angels. But I couldn't wait to leave. I looked longingly down the road and dreamed of adventure in the city. Since I left the farm to become a writer, I've slept an ever-more bookish sleep of the idle thinker. It's been a long while since the deeply satisfying physical slumber of my straw-hand childhood.

I was born a fifth-generation John on the land settled deep in southwestern Ontario by my great-great-grandfather and namesake, Irish John Lee. I betrayed my heritage and left the farm at eighteen to pursue a career as a teacher and a poet. I'd thought to leave behind the dreary labours of my

9

youth and yet it haunts my work and is not quite so dreary in recall. I thought I lived at the centre of nowhere. I've learned since then that there is no such a place. Nowhere is a state of mind. Contrary to my suspicions, I'd lived a fascinating and privileged childhood. Everything I know about the world, I learned on the land. The farm on the hill I called home lives on in my most vivid imaginings of a private past. If, as someone once said, "It is memory that keeps us sane," then I owe the sanity of my life to my childhood as a farmer's son. This is but a little taste from the flavour of that childhood. Though I left the farm on the hill I once called home, almost everything I know can be measured between the railway line running the far acres of the back fields by the bush and oak to the south, and the Gosnell line to the north and the village farm east and the neighbour's farm west where I once watched ten thousand swans fly down to rest like snowfall on the till as far as I could see into the distance.

Sunset Outside of Shannon
on Our Last Night in Ireland

IN THE SUMMER of 1994 three generations of my family and I returned to Ireland, the land of my ancestors. On the last evening of our visit to the old country, my father and I sat on the lawn looking west to sunfall shadowed on the green fields well outside of city Shannon. The laundered B&B bedding flapped on the line in the foreground like sheets full of wind from ships of passage. It was a lovely evening, quiet with the cool warm breath of the world. My thoughts were of the bitter-sweet sort we feel when things are so nearly perfect they almost wound us with their beauty. This was the end of our sojourn. Tomorrow we would fly home. My parents would remember this trip as the best of their lives. My mother still lingers over the photographs of us all on the Island that our forebears had left the century before.

I sat in the sad and looked to my father who watched the dusk fall in the far and I wondered what he thought.

"What are you thinking about, Dad?" I asked him, hoping he'd say that to him this failing light was a common covenant and this country we'd seen was the best.

"I'm thinking of home, son," he said and he sighed. "I'm thinking, no matter how lovely this place, it doesn't hold a candle to Canada. I'm thinking of the farm where I live and how much more beautiful it is even than this."

And so it has always been for him. I'd heard him say the same before and I've heard him say the same a dozen times since then. I've overheard those very words spoken to a stranger he'd met as he sat on a bench near the Spanish market in Los Angeles. I've heard his conviction on the steps of Capital Hill in Washington and I've heard it overlooking the great Pacific ocean from the tar-sand beach of Carpinteria, California with the coastal mountain Christmas majesty looming behind us. He loves the land he was born to most and best.

Two years ago when he and I and mother sat on the home veranda at the farm, looking out at the blue heavens where a double rainbow bent horizon to horizon before us, my father said, "Isn't it wonderful to think how this same sky was seen by my great-grandfather before the land was cleared? I'm the luckiest man in the world," he'd said, meaning "here," meaning "being here now," meaning "being home, born at home, living at home, and growing old with the prospect of being here forever, connected to this life by knowing this place, knowing his place in the world, fixed exactly here on this very farm." To him, this house, these barns, these familiar acres were indeed better than all other places.

Others might ask, "But how do you know, George? You've never lived anywhere else." Others might wonder, but not he. These one-hundred-and-thirty fecund acres of land in the heart of southwestern Ontario bring him as close to the Garden as any man might come. His house, the only house he's ever known, is a perfect homely paradise. This year, he's off to cruise the Amazon. He's reading about Brazil. I'm sure he'll tell the captain where he lives and why. He'll cross the burning line with pictures in his wallet he'll gladly show to strangers in the sub-equatorial heat, while winter freezes the water at the barn and my uncle shovels his way to the truck from the door.

"I wish I were home," he will say, "I wish I were home."

Everything I Know About Literature
I Learned on the Farm

I AM A POET, not a farmer, though I was born a farmer's son. I spent the first nineteen years of my life on the very land settled by my great-great-grandfather and namesake, John Lee. His was fertile earth deep in the heart of what would come to be known as southwestern Ontario.

Whenever I visit the farm where I was born and raised, I am painfully aware that important things are slowly coming to a close. For my father has passed and my mother and uncle are growing old and slowing down. I need only regard the fading glory of the prize plaques in the sheep pen, and the black paint shaling from the failing barns with their sagging whitewashed stone foundations to know I am right. And when I see the crisis coming concerning what to do with the land, I realize that I have betrayed my parentage by leaving. However, I have always felt something of a foundling in me. I was never qualified to stay, despite my consanguinary obligations. My roots are deep in the land of my father and the land is deep in me. So, what to do? I am no tiller, nor have I ever been. I was born to books.

My earth is made from paper. My plough turns a furrow of words. I am the fifth John Lee. I honour my ancestors with poems and stories. I look to the photographs of the original John, my progenitor. I see in his eyes, and the homely jaw-whiskers of his face, in the thin grim line of his mouth, an approval. My poems are a good crop. They arise from the earth he tilled. Everything I know about literature began with what I learned on the farm and from the farm. Many of the words I write are ancestor worship, and they arise from an acute awareness of my duty to John Lee and the generations he sired.

Before becoming an emigrant pioneer, John Lee, born March 5, 1803, had been a teacher in Cork, Ireland. According to the book, *Shorthorn Cattle in Canada*, he arrived in 1828, a young college man from the Old Land. He took official possession of the deed of the farm on the hill near Highgate, on August 8th, 1854 for the price and sum of forty three pounds, fifteen shillings.

My Uncle John tells me that a landholder must, within the first year of his having taken possession of his acres, build a house which measures twelve by twelve. The intention was to require shelter and encourage family. Some devious pioneers cheated the system by building in inches rather than feet, constructing a dwelling 12" by 12", thereby being in compliance with the letter of the law if not the spirit of the law. What was little more than a log doll-house or shanty for a small dog or bothy for the skunks satisfied the exact instructions of the clergy reserve—a good roof over a lazy woodchuck and nothing more.

It was there on the farm that Irish John's first son John was born in late winter. This John Lee, known locally as "Big" John Lee, prospered as a farmer. And though there have been sheep on the farm since 1851, John would bring the first purebred longwool Lincoln Sheep over from the old country in 1889 and thereby begin to establish what was to become one of the best flocks of Lincolns in North America. He would go on to serve as a Liberal MLA at Toronto for two terms just after the turn of the century. His son, Herb, began exhibiting sheep at local, national and international shows in 1910 and thus would begin the tradition which would make the Lee family the only family to have exhibited livestock at the Royal Winter Fair every year since its inception. This fact would result in Herb's son John being honoured as a dinner guest at the Royal and give him the opportunity for a fifteen minute audience with Princess Anne of the House of Windsor.

Despite this proud heritage as the only and last male in a long line of Lee's on the land, I have always been in every way unfit to take on the farm. Should I scribe a circle with a fifty kilometre radius, and thereby take in Chatham, Cedar Springs, and Morpeth, I would include in that circumference two important poets and one impressive county history: Archibald Lampman and Raymond Knister and the book, *Romantic Kent*. I did not study Lampman in school, nor did I read Knister before the publication of *Windfalls for Cider: The Poems of Raymond Knister*, in 1983, though there was always a copy of *Romantic Kent* in our library at home. Before I was old enough to cut the pages of that tome, I saw it on the shelf of the bookcase in the parlour and wondered at its massive romance.

I think I must have been born a writer. Long before I started school, I was opening big books and scribbling with a pencil on the pages, yearning to know what writing was. There are still five of six important books I might pull down to see the scrawl of my yearning there. I wrote before I knew how to write. I did not love the tractors though I loved the tractor fumes. The smell of gasoline on the winter wind can still evoke memories in me of sitting on my father's lap behind the engine housing of the old orange Case and riding the chill back the lane to the field. And yet, I never struck a single furrow in all my years at home. I never cultivated corn. I could not be trusted.

On the other hand, my grandfather nicknamed me "Sigh-cow-ski" because I wore the recording of *Sleeping Beauty* smooth from listening over and over again on the old crank-up Victrola. I remember being the brunt of his joke as he scrawled the word, "Aristophanes" on the little children's chalk board on the wall beside the bathroom, saying to the five-year-old pre-schooler he'd taught to read and print, "say that word, Johnny," and then laughing at me when I sounded it out "air-iss-toe-fanes." I may not have been able to drive the standard-shift truck the way my cousin Stuart could before he could even reach the pedals. I may not have loved being at the barns the way other farmer's sons would because the work was there. But I knew by heart the stories my aunt Stella would tell about the war. I loved the poems of Edgar A. Guest my dad would read with smiling eyes. I loved to wander the fields and tell myself tales of winter wars on the Plains of Abraham.

I walked a mile to school and when I walked alone, I re-created for myself the fall of the Roman Empire. I dreamed myself a soldier in Caesar's armies on the march through Gaul. I talked of Achilles and the sacking of Troy. I marched and lay siege on Moscow in my great-coat with my maple branch musket. When I was old enough, I worked with our hired hand Tom Malott, stooking grain, cutting corn, hoeing beans, handling hay and listening closely to his words. The Lees were strange and I was lucky. I lived in a house and ate at a table rich with story. My grandfather, my uncle, the hired man, my sister, mother, father and I at every meal. I didn't know it then, in fact I didn't know it until well after I'd begun to write, that I was learning the stories it was given me to tell.

That Tom Malott was hung upside down in the well by his father who punished him that way for wetting the bed; that my grandfather Herb Lee would bury the ashes of his blue-haired sister with these words, shaking her urn next to his ear at her graveside, "Mabel, Mabel, are you in there Mabel?"; that my aunt Stella would tell us again and again how the German prisoners of war were brought to work on the farm, and how one soldier would point and say in broken English to my grandmother, "Is that your son?", meaning the young man in the navy uniform in the photograph in the dining room, and he would weep to know; that I would play hockey on the flooded fields in the burning winds of winter and write of that; that I would see the gulls behind my harrow and feel connected years later to the gulls I saw following the fishing boats of Lunenburg; that I grew up near Buxton and the Dawn settlements, and found I was descended from Harriet Beecher Stowe who based her character of Uncle Tom upon Josiah Henson of Dresden, and that I would write of that, and also of John Brown who planned his raid on Harper's Ferry in my nearby city, the city of Chatham on the Thames; and that Al Purdy would write his last poem, "Ya Gotta Know Yer Can Lit," in which he would quote my title for those poems, "Kicheraboo, We are Dying"; that I would hear my mother say, "Tippecanoe and Tyler too," and would only learn years later that I was also descended from President Tyler, the only president in the history of the United States who ever gave up his citizenship, and that the phrase referred to the election campaign of president William Henry Harrison, who led the American forces at the Battle of the Thames where Tecumseh fell, and who had also driven Tecumseh out of his home state of Ohio as a result of Harrison having won the battle of Tippecanoe; and that I was also descended by way of my Gosnell blood from Captain Bartholomew Gosnold who was instrumental in establishing the first permanent English colony in North America at Jamestown; that Highgate was known as the Gosnell settlement, and was thus connected to Jamestown and to Bartholomew's cousin Henry who was Queen's Counsel in Ireland to Elizabeth the First, thus making a genealogical line connecting us to Raleigh, Bacon, Beecher, Tyler, leading me to conclude that everything is everything and there is no such place as nowhere—even William Shakespeare's great play, *The Tempest*, traces its origins to accounts of Gosnold's first voyage on the Concord; that I would think of the impact on cows of listening to the inter-planetary blues of Jimi Hendrix and write a sound poem which Much Music would turn into a video, and Virgin Records would record, and which I would perform before an audience of two thousand delighted people on the Stuart McLean show, *Vinyl Café*, a show which would be replayed several times over the course of a year; that the farm boy who woke up one day when he saw the Beatles on television in February 1964, and thereby would leave the land forever, though he didn't know it then; that the boy who husbanded his father's herd of purebred Shorthorn cattle so they won premier breeder at Western Fair in 1969 would go on to write *The Bad Philosophy of Good Cows* and *The Black Barns Trilogy*; that I would turn my disqualifiers—the times I fell through mow holes, the time I lost the gravity box on the railway tracks, the time I took my wether into a ewe class, the time I was dragged a quarter mile by the Poppy heifer in front of the grand stand at Ridgetown Fair, the ways I could neither hammer a nail nor fix an engine, the fact that I was indifferent to automobiles, and couldn't care less about the crops, though I loved the rotten gold of over-ripe wheat, and the crushed sow circles of heavy winds in the oats; it amazes me how long it took for it to occur to me to write the farm. To take the stories and mine my youth for gold.

In 1986, with the publication of *Hired Hands*, I finally came to write the first of a series of books arising from the stories it was given me to tell. And subsequent poems are rooted in that place I would leave behind in 1970 at the age of eighteen when I went off to university in London. Even the poems which aren't about the farm benefit from what I learned by living there. The words, clevis, gambrel, stooking, the experience of the hog-killing tree and the scalding shed, the sense of the well and deep waters, the idea of being a guardian of this place we inhabit, of making improvements, of our duty to honour the past and consider the future, these are my inheritance. I may have left the land, I may have failed my father, I may have betrayed my ancestors by leaving to become a poet, but I am not a farmer, though I was born a farmer's son.

And I feel the heat of Lampman's fields, and I follow Knister's plough knowing as he knew and wrote these lines in his poem, "The Plowman," "some day, some day, be sure/ I shall turn the furrow of all my hopes/ But I shall not, doing it, look back." But I do look back upon my share to see how blessed I am to know the things I know about a place. And as Souwesto's premier professor and poet James Reaney advises us to learn our world—I can name the weeds and crops; I can wick the dogbane in the beans, I can write the "L" of the farmhouse veranda. I can tell cow from cow, and call the barrow what he is for all lack-sex of his gender-loss. I know my capon and my steer, my mouton, wether, eanling, shoat and gilt. I can see the connection between the hog on the hoof and the candied Sunday-dinner ham. I can see how the ram scrotum swings among thistles and not be squeamish to compare. I laugh and know exactly what my father means when he refers to a barrow as a 'gentleman who has lost his standing in the community in which he resides.'

Old Farm, New Farm

THE BUILDINGS ON our farm have always attracted the attention of photographers. Set on the crest of a hill three-tenths of a mile from the road, they have appeared in a variety of newspapers at least a half a dozen times. *The Windsor Star*, *The London Free Press*, *The Chatham Daily News*, *The Ridgetown Dominion*, *The Independent*, and several farming journals all in their day have assigned photographers the task of capturing the majesty and beauty of those barns from the road. They have always shown especially well in the spring with the lambs on the grass, or in winter when the front mucks had flooded wide as two ten-acre lakes running west to east and diked in the centre by the divide of the farm lane.

When I was a boy, the barns had been red, the tin roofs silver and the foundations and foregrounded silo lime-wash white for decades. I've been told that in the early days of agriculture in this province the paint was tinted crimson with the blood of slaughtered animals. Until recently red has been the colour favoured by farmers for their outbuildings all over Ontario countryside. One might see a rare green tobacco kiln, or a white dairy building painted that milk shade often preferred by the owners of the Friesian breed. But red signified the prosperity of my own rural youth.

Like many well-to-do and proud country folk, we own an aerial photograph of the place from those days with the red, red-roan, and pure white Shorthorn cattle dotting the pastures, along with the good-land Lincolns set like clouds in the green where the brown rivers of their walking trails flowed away from the water-barrels and grain troughs set out near the gates. Those twelve buildings and that single silo of Leeland Farms make a lovely silver-roofed, red-cedared rectangle from the sky.

The big barn with its fieldstone foundation, the new barn, the little old barn, brick barn, ram's pen, bull's pen, sheep pen, granary, hen house, implement shed, gutting shed, pump house and two houses make an all from the air framed by a pine stand, hundred-year maple, elm and oak, and fenced fields road to railway, neighbour to neighbour.

The red barns were last freshened in the centennial year, when government money became available for improvements made by farm families 100 years or more on the same land. Now the barns are shaled black, the faded red blushing through from 1967. My father had first seen black barns with green rooves at a Shorthorn Breeders' picnic. He was so struck by the stark beauty of black barns he immediately resolved to paint the cedar siding black. He came home and hired the crew to change the colour. Indeed the buildings did become an even more striking sight, set on the hill in black and green. That was over thirty years ago. A second aerial photograph larger than the first hangs in a place of honour in the dining room of the brick house. It captures the full splendour of our farm as seen from the sky.

And those buildings have attracted the attention not only of photographers, but of artists as well. Sculptor and visual artist Michel Binet had left Quebec in the early seventies and was travelling the secondary roads of southwestern Ontario looking for a place to settle and to improve his command of English. On his journey, he drove the Gosnell line running east and west between the village of Highgate and the town of Ridgetown fronting our farm to the north. He could not pass those barns on the hill without stopping and driving in. He was struck by their beauty. He drove up the lane, took several photographs and brief studies of the place. He also fixed his mind upon finding somewhere to live in Kent. He settled upon a converted schoolhouse near Thamesville and set up his studio there. He began to paint canvases of the farm, the house, and a bent-wood bark-seat chair he'd seen on our porch. He also did several portraits of our hired man, Tom, whom he'd met that first fortuitous visit.

In 1984 I was writing *Hired Hands*, a book about our farmhand, Tom Malott. When I gave a copy of the manuscript to my mother and father for Christmas, my mom said, "John, did you know there's a local artist who has done paintings of Tom? He lives in a converted schoolhouse near here. You should go and visit him." I drove over to Michel's and he showed me all his work. He'd already sold the painting of the house. He'd also sold a painting of Tom's fiddle sitting in the bent-wood bark-seat chair to a restaurant in Ridgetown. He'd done one watercolour, one pencil sketch and two ink drawings of Tom. In the pencil drawing Tom is sitting on the top step in the doorway leading to the barnyard. He's wearing an old fedora Michel had found in Tom's bedroom.

More recently, I had the honour of showing off our place to two talented photographers. My dad was a little hesitant to agree because the outbuildings have fallen into disrepair since they've sat empty for the last five years since the livestock have been sold. This visit coincided with the presence of a portion of the world-famous Highgate Mastadon which was on display in the village library. My father thought it a perfect opportunity for the visiting artists to take photographs of the bones and tusks of the ice age creature.

The two photographers arrived in good light, shared a cup of tea in the house and went to the barns. I told Dad to leave them be and let them wander and take photographs wherever they wished. I know Dad was a little embarrassed by the dishevelment of the buildings. The cattle trough was cracked and broken, the fieldstone foundation of the largest barn was tumbling loose, the mow boards were wowed with hay, the silo was sealed with a poisonous gas warning, and worst of all, a dead raccoon hung from the eave at the end of the barn thirty feet from the ground. My father had not noticed. That dead raccoon seemed almost alive up-there mid-leap like a taxidermist's high-wire act.

The men took photographs of cobwebby windows, mouse-eaten smocks on nails, old pails turned over in the dust, paint cans cluttered with stiff-bristled brushes, crack-leather halters hanging from spikes, rusted machinery left overlong in the rain, empty sheep sheds shaling into ruin. My father was saying, "if only you'd seen this farm when it was a show place." I knew he was mortified by the state of things. My uncle had been bringing home clutter from barn sales for the last decade. Every space was a nuisance ground of bicycle skeletons and broken machines. Old washing machine agitation drums sat beside weird inter-galactic, flying-saucer-seeming silo covers. The cameras clicked and captured deterioration in the full glory of its character. I know and understand my father's point of view. I can recall when the barns were fresh, the grass was groomed, and the gravel was peppered with sheep dung and scattered with apples. For all that, the photographers were interested only in the character of a farm in ruin. I remember as a boy being fascinated by the tall orchard grass sweeping the base of the windmill at my maternal great-grandfather's farm. There's beauty in things gone to seed. The wind waltzing the soft green sweep of uncut grass and the broken struts of the windmill half-turning in the heights were both beautiful. The eye loves a gentle wreckage of man-made things returning to the earth. My father wanted to leave the impression that this farm was once a prosperous and busy working operation with the straw still gold from harvest, not this etiolated brown over-used broom-coloured stuff that sheds from the broken old stack. These two wanted sloven and sag, shale and waste.

Let weeds bring down the barns. Let wind have the hollows. The clapboard house where I was born is falling into beauty. The skunks and raccoons inhabit the rooms. Look in through the windows to where they've made their nests. I was once a toddler there. My first memories have broken faith with time.

An Absence of Houses

WERE YOU TO regard the farm from the summer road, you might indeed wonder at the whereabouts of a single house, when there are in fact three houses. The clinker-built and the large brick are both obscured from view by a stand of pine and thick young undergrowth of weed maples which make an arboreal camouflage against a clear view, a sort of palisade, a wall of trees in which there are also two full-grown maples, a swing tree and a tap-spiled sugar which has never yielded a single drop of sap for syrup. The third house is also the first original framed dwelling. It dates from a fire which destroyed all but the back kitchen. This kitchen was removed from its place to where it served first as a hen coop, then as a farrowing pen. It now sits empty of purpose. It holds several sets of stale encyclopedia bought at estate sales and left there as a library for rodents.

If you were to look very closely at the grey tongue-in-groove interior walls and ceiling, you might glimpse the last cracking of wallpaper still clinging to the wood. The house was mostly burned when my grandfather's sister Mabel was smoking in bed. That fire gave rise to the brick which now stands as the last occupied house on the farm.

Built before my father was born, this two-story, six-bedroom dwelling is the pride of the farm. It was constructed doubly strong. My grandfather had witnessed the collapse of a parlour when a poorly made home had fallen floor to earth under the weight of grief at a wake.

The mourners went crashing through the floor to the basement like the giving way of ice. The brick house remains relatively poorly served by electricity because my grandfather did not trust that it would not kindle a fire in the wall. He believed the outlets would spontaneously overheat, combust and ignite the lath like moisture trapped in grain.

So there are no outlets upstairs and only a few down. There are none in the four bedrooms or in the upstairs hall. There is none in the den, only one in the dining room, two in the parlour, two in the kitchen and none in the bathroom. When I wanted to play my records as a boy, I had to screw in a socket outlet above the lightbulb and plug into that. Even a simple cool-air fan blew a fuse. Sleeping upstairs on hot summer nights was like the dark torpor of a fever room.

The other house, the smaller clapboard home, was my first. It had been brought to the farm through the village by team and sled around 1919. That house was first brought to our land to accommodate a hired hand and his bride. Ben Tunstall was a man from England who worked for my grandfather. His bride, Alice, was a Barnardo girl, brought here to help my grandmother in the kitchen. Ben and Alice's five children were born and raised in that house. Ben died there. After his death, Alice moved to the village and my father brought his own bride, my mother, Lillian Irene Lee, née Busteed, home to start their family there. They were married January 8th, 1949. My sister was born to that home in 1950 and I was born in 1951. We lived in that house for the first three years of my life.

I have only a very few recollections from those early years. I have been told that one day, my sister was playing on the kitchen floor when my mother heard her calling, 'here kitty, kitty'. As there were no cats allowed indoors, my mother's attention was attracted by the kitty call. She was startled to discover that my sister's attention was in fact attracted by a rat which had come up from the dirt-floor cellar to scout for food in the kitchen cupboards. That perhaps explains the presence of rat traps I've seen hanging from their hinges in the gutting shed. A wiser and an older girl might have importuned the rodent with, "here ratty, ratty." I am left to imagine my mother scooping up her thus-endangered daughter and my father setting traps for another rat-fatal day. As for me, I never saw a rat in that house.

My first memory dates from my second year on this planet. I had been given a boy doll as a gift by someone. I plunged him head first, hair cut to chin, in my night-soiled potty like a plumber's dirty work. For that faecal dunking I received my first spanking as my mother swatted my diapered hind end.

The second memory of that house involved the placing of a snow-fence-perimeter around our yard. My sister and I had toddled off unattended and made our way down the lane to play in the middle of the road. We were found there playing hot-tar pebble bounce by some passerby who put us in his car and brought us home to our horrified mother. My father immediately put up a six-foot snow fence which caged us in the yard. Someone took a photograph of my sister and me peering like convicts through shadow, looking mournfully at the world beyond the slats.

My third memory arises from the day I'd fallen from the wagon wrack onto the wagon tongue thereby breaking my leg. "A green break," the doctor would call it because of how it resembled the spiral splintering of a young tree branch with too much sap in the stem. My uncle, who had been driving the tractor, had been out gathering fresh corn stalks for cattle feed. He brought me home broken-legged and handed me over to my mother.

That evening, after being in pain all afternoon, I sat on the chesterfield being coached across parlour linoleum by my father who was saying to me, "Walk to me. You can walk to me. Your leg's not broken. Come on, walk." Try as I might, I could not cross that difficult water-patterned distance for my leg was indeed broken.

In 1955, just after my grandmother was diagnosed with diabetes and a weakened heart, we moved into the brick house and grandma and grandpa moved into the smaller frame house. The reason for the move, as I have been told, was that my grandmother was too ill to care for such a large home. My sister, mother, and father and I moved in to live with Tom, the hired man, and my father's brother, Uncle John. Tom occupied the bedroom across the hall from mine, and Uncle John slept in the bedroom across the hall from my sister, Georgina.

My bedroom had been my father and uncle's bedroom as boys. I smelled the clock oil and the smoke from trump cigars wafting from Tom's bedroom. I heard the deep resonance of my father's voice through the wood of the floor from the bedroom below my own. Tom lived in a room alive with the ticking of clocks. His dresser drawers were full of clock parts. He had one cuckoo clock on his wall, and about a dozen alarm clocks all working at once. His bedroom ticked like a jewellery shop. He also owned about four or five pocket watches fobbed on boot laces.

My grandmother died a year or so after the move. I have only two recollections of her alive. In one I am on her lap picking my nose and she is slapping my hand and saying, "Don't do that! It's a filthy habit." In another, my sister and I went over to visit and have supper. Grandma made macaroni and cheese. Her macaroni was uncommonly crimson. I suppose she must have made it with too much ketchup for my palate. And then, she died.

I spent the next seven years sharing table with six people. My grandfather, my Uncle John, and Tom joined the four of us at every meal, though Grandpa usually came quite late to breakfast. "We never had a home of our own," my mother said. But to me this was home, and I never knew nor ever wished for another.

Grandpa stayed alone in the frame house. In the kitchen, there was a tin cupboard occupied by a solitary, unopened box of breakfast cereal. When he was still well enough to get around, I'd often find him sitting at his kitchen table writing letters. Years later when I was writing a book about him, my cousin from the west sent me a parcel of correspondence between him and her older sister, Hila. I suppose that he might have been writing those very epistles from when I was visiting as a little boy. Hila had squirrelled them away in the piano bench in Regina and her sister sent them to me to help me to know my grandpa when I was writing that book.

Grandpa slept upstairs until he took his first fall. His bed was surrounded by newspapers to catch his tobacco spit. My city cousin told me recently they had to spread newspapers on the broadloom whenever he paid them a visit. The headboard of his bed was scarred by a tear-drop-shaped scorch mark where he struck wooden lucifers to light his pipe. The bed-side table held a milky-watered drinking glass where he'd float his dentures while he slept. Sometimes when I'd visit him there, I was given the chore of gathering up the crusty newspapers littered with blackened matchends. I'd be required to put down fresh papers as if I were about to paint the room.

In the last year of his life, he fell and injured his leg so that he had difficulty walking. That lead to a rapid decline in his health. He moved to the downstairs bedroom at the back of the house. That room quickly came to resemble the room upstairs. A clutter of books leaned left and right on the dresser top and tossed down newspapers breathed from the floor and stuck to your shoe bottoms when you walked towards his bed. My sister and I brought his meals to him on a black wicker tray. I thought of that tray as the sickness tray, because we only used it when someone was bedridden by illness.

For almost a full year, my grandfather stayed in bed. I'd take him his meals, help him to his toilet, stay there and talk a while, and ruffle through the books to borrow the best. Although he did not read novels because he had "no time for lying," most of the books he had in the room were novels lent to him by his daughter Stella. Stella had a passion for fiction. Many of the books there were WWII bodice rippers. The one book I read from that pile which I liked the most was *The Moon is Down*, a WWII novel by John Steinbeck.

I remember the morning after he'd died in the night. My father took him his supper and he'd eaten heartily. After a long spell of poor appetite, he'd said, "I'm beginning to feel a little better, George. Could you ask Irene to make me a big breakfast." In the morning, Dad found him cold. I heard his simple heartfelt words through the closed den door, "Dad's gone." And then, his gentle tears.

That was the first of many human deaths I witnessed up close. My feelings were a strange mixture of curiosity, relief, shame and grief. For my sister, the farm remains haunted by those who have died in the rooms of those houses. How many spirits linger in the wainscot or rest on the sills of the windows? Enough I suppose to link the glass-rattle of hard winter weather with the spirits of the dead.

Only yesterday I heard a story about yet another house on the farm. A log cabin occupied a small ridge under the old orchard just west of the clapboard house. When my grandfather was a little boy, there were sometimes up to ten or twenty natives camping there. The last occupant of that log house was a shaman of the Potawatomi. She lived there until one day when she was very old she called upon her family to take her to the lake. When she arrived at the waters of Lake Erie, she simply walked out and disappeared into the depths of the lake. This land is a deep tell of those who have gone before us. There is much to learn from the story of what has disappeared. The Potawatomi woman came with her clan from Michigan, arriving in the region after the Americans drove them from their own land south of the border. The Attawandaron lived on the northern shores of the lake until the mid-seventeenth century. The most-complete mastodon skeleton ever unearthed is called The Highgate Mastodon. Purchased by an American, it is kept in a museum in the States. Though the fences are down and the buildings are falling into serious disrepair, I know that time goes on and things will change. I think back to the first log cabin, the first frame house, the first felled trees, the last wild bear, the last remaining shaman shack, the last cleared field, these all are visible only to the inner eye and available only to a vivid imagining.

My grandfather cleared the front muck last of all the fields on the farm when he was a young man. When a passing neighbour stopped to chat with him on a day when he was plowing those wet acres, he said, "Now I know how the Israelites felt crossing the parting of the Red Sea." And thus he fixed his place in time in the great foreverness of distant past and forthcoming future. He walked the soft black till of that day, following the plough which would one day follow the tractor of his sons.

In a last letter to his cousin Hila, he wrote of himself, "I'm not yet ready for the worms." However morbid those words might seem to some, I think of the appetite of those long-since satiated worms and know my grandfather meant it as a natural thought. He placed himself in the continuum of dust and ashes. He used to love to talk of God with his friend the Reverend Cross. His God was the God of the cycles of the seasons and the weather on the land. He's buried in the earth becoming earth. His spirit enriches the loam.

Hired Hands

THE YEAR I WAS born, Thomas Sheil Malott was in his early fifties. He had come to our farm to seek work as a hired hand when he was but a boy of twelve. He was there living with us when my father was just a lad and he was still there working when I left home to attend university in London. Mostly an odd-chores man, he remained until he was worked out. Roughly a decade after I left home permanently, he developed a sore on his foot that would not heal. The raw spot on his skin was the result of his rubber boots rubbing the flesh till it blistered and when the blister broke, it became infected, making it necessary for Tom to go to the doctor. He ended up in hospital where he remained convalescent for several days. The doctor suggested he be removed from there and taken directly to a nursing-care facility.

By that time he was in his early eighties and the doctor said to my father, "If you take him home to the farm, George, you had better be prepared to nurse him till he dies. Better that he go where his needs can be met, now that he's accustomed to being away from home."

Tom stayed there in that nursing home overlooking the Thames river in Chatham for the rest of his days. I had thought he would miss the farm and pine away to return. He did not. I thought he would miss his freedom. He did not. He spent most days sitting in a chair in the visiting room quietly smoking his pipe. He seemed quite content to be absolutely inactive. In the last year of his life he had a stroke which left him morbid, mumbling, dull, and weepy. Every time I went to visit he wept. I have been told this is not uncommon for stroke victims. Some become violent. Some quiet. Some lugubrious. And Tom was the latter. He became inconsolable. He wept like dog-loss at every visit. Even the word, "tractor" would make him grieve quietly into his hand.

When I was very young, I put one of my mother's sayings to the test. "Tom would argue black is white," I'd heard her say with exasperation. Being a slightly precocious five-year-old who knew his colours, whereas, Tom did not, "Tom," I said to him there in our country kitchen. "Black is not a colour."

"Tis so!" Tom said. "Any fool knows that." Tom said.

"No, Tom," I said. "Black is not a colour. Black is the absence of colour. And," I continued, "White is not a colour either."

"Yes it is," said Tom. I did not yet notice the signs I would later learn to read as warnings like the hackles of a dog, the tail lashings of a cat, the foreleg stamping of a ram, the pawing of a bull. Tom's jaw was beginning to set, his fists to clench, his arms to stiffen.

"No, Tom," I said. "White is not a colour. White is the presence of all the colours in the spectrum." I said. "Therefore," I said. "Black is not a colour. White is not a colour. Therefore, black is not white." I said. Thus I concluded. Thus he closed his fist and hit me.

"Goddamn kid. Don't know nothin'." I'd heard him say something similar before about those he did not like—men who made fun of him because he could neither read nor write; men who belittled him because he thought Leamington was the farthest away it was possible to go for he'd never been beyond Leamington which was a mere fifty miles away.

"Goddamn kid don't know nothin'." I knew he regretted hitting me. Not that he thought he'd be fired for it, but he genuinely regretted hitting me because he was not a man prone to violence. In fact, he was kind and gentle and loving and good.

I learned a lesson. I learned not to tease Tom. I learned not to be too smart for my own good. I learned that all arrogance is foolish and all arrogant men are fools. I did not want this man to hit me again. More to the point, I did not want to hurt him. I was five and I loved this man. I loved him till he died.

The day of his funeral, I sat in the grieving room reserved for the family and loved ones. I heard his voice clear and true above the drone of the organ, "Boysees it's cold, Johnny," and I also heard the hand clap that warmed him in winter over the blue flames of the gas range in the kitchen. His voice was so distinct, I wondered that no one else seemed to hear it. "Boysees it's cold Johnny," and the snap of his palms cracking together like lonely applause.

He'd first come to our farm because he had run away from home. He was just a child on the road. "He'd been pushed from pillar to post," was the way my dad had put it. He fled his own family because his stepfather had abused him. He'd hung him upside down in the farm well for wetting the bed. Tom's half-brother had rescued him and beaten his father up. Tom ran off, never to return, working here and there until he arrived on our land to be given a home by my grandfather, Herb. I heard the story of Tom's punishment from Tom when he was in a story-telling mood. "If I ever see him again, I'll kill the bastard!" Tom would say of his stepfather, setting his jaw on the resolution.

Tom was the last in a long line of hired help. At one point, my grandfather had nine men working on the farm. When my great-grandfather, John Lee, was a member of parliament in the early years of the twentieth century, the need of his spending time in Toronto made it necessary for a full-time hired man to work while he fulfilled his duties as an elected official.

Jim T., a young bachelor from Scotland, was our first hired hand. He offered his services to my great-grandfather. The arrangement was that he would be paid one-hundred-and-ten dollars per annum, but rather than draw the total amount, John Lee would pay him only what he needed for clothing, tobacco, and the courting of his bride to be. The remainder of his stipend would be set aside to be paid at the end of his service. Four years after this agreement, Jim was given the three-hundred-and-sixty dollars owed to him for his four years of service. He had spent only eighty dollars in four years.

The next hired hand for whom I have any record, was John Daily Smith who was rendering service in gratitude and by way of repayment for having been taken in as an orphan. So the story goes, he lived with my great-aunt Catherine Shehan, who had marrried a man named Daily. Out of deference to the generosity of his adoptive parents, the boy, John Smith, chose to call himself "John Daily Smith." He worked on the farm until at the age of sixteen he left to make his fortune. This boy is of special interest to me because he is the grandfather of my mother's mother. It wasn't until after my mother and father were married, that Mom learned of the connection.

John Daily Smith, my mother's great-grandfather, bought land near the lake. He farmed a farm across the road from a sand strip known locally as Terrace Beach. In the last years of her life, my grandmother went blind. We took her for a picnic along the lake and while we were sunbathing and feeling the slight postprandial fatigue of summer, she took my arm and said, "I'd like to see the place where I watered my grandfather's horses as a little girl." We stepped gingerly along the strand with her holding my arm, arriving where the cold stream crossed the road threading into Lake Erie. "This is the spot," she said, remembering herself as a child with her grandfather's thirsty horses. Later when I talked to my mother about that day, she said, "Didn't you know that your grandmother's grandfather was raised on the Lee farm?" And she told me the story of that coincidental connection.

John Lee's son Herb, born in 1876, left the farm as a young man to run cattle and sheep from England to the Argentine. He made two successful journeys and then a third which would prove a failure. He returned to the home farm which he bought from his father after four years away.

When he was a boy, Herb used to play with the native children who had a cabin under the walnut orchard near the garden next to the where the other house now stands. My great-grandfather often hired natives as temporary hands to help out in shocking the corn or during the hog-killing bees.

The killing bee was a communal activity which involved the slaughter of animals and the preparation of the meat for winter. The Indians helped in the day's work and would each receive a severed pig's head as payment. This satisfied for many years until one bee, when an Indian who had served in the army during the First World War approached John, noticeably disappointed with the offered pig's head. He came cap in hand, politely and quietly saying, "John, since I've been to war, I've become used to eating a little further back on the hog."

The next hired man I know of was Ben Tunstall. He arrived at our farm as a young man. He fell in love with Alice, a Barnardo girl working for my grandmother and helping out in the house. They married in 1919 and my grandfather moved a house onto our land where they would live for next thirty-two years. My father, born in 1922, has very fond memories of growing up with Ben and Alice's children as playmates and best friends. At the same time as Ben was there, my grandfather also hired John Squires and Charlie Burchette. Ben became a sort of foreman for these two. Ben was a good man and always cheerful. My father fondly remembers his daily greeting, "Good morning. Lovely morning this morning." Rain or shine. Overcast or clear. Stormy or still. Every weather had its charm in the cheerful life of Ben Tunstall.

John Squires was called an 'off again, on again' hand because he would come and go as he pleased, borrowing the family pony, Tiny, to take buggy trips at his leisure.

Charlie Burchette, to quote my father, was 'a crazy little Frenchman,' cruelly nicknamed Charlie Birdshit by my father and his brother John. Charlie was a real character with a bad temper and a foul mouth who needed constant supervision without which he would do nothing. My father remembers playing pranks on Charlie. One time they switched his handlebars and bicycle seat around so he couldn't figure out how to ride the damn contraption. Charlie got so mad he hit my father who beat him so badly that he said, "I would have killed him if someone hadn't hauled me off." One time Charlie said something rude and insulting to my grandmother in the kitchen and my grandfather picked him up by the scruff of the neck and the seat of the pants and hurled him head first through the closed window so he came down in the yard in shards of glass clattering like strange weather. Charlie ended up in a mental institution after biting someone's hand on the streets of Chatham. He died a mad, broken man hurling curses at the world.

Bill Green was a remittance man whom Uncle John remembers because he used to play fiddle and sing "Big Rock Candy Mountain" at the top of his lungs while he relaxed in the evenings after the daily chores. It was once quite common for well-to-do English families to send misfit children overseas with a small allowance. They were usually exiled because they were an embarrassment at home. Bill Green was such a man. My uncle remembers him fondly as an able worker and as an especially entertaining performer .

Willis Geddis worked on our farm annually during the haying season. He was a narcissist with a well-groomed beard, who prided himself in his intelligence, wit, strength and virtuous character. Like most braggarts, he was far from the perfect specimen he thought himself to be. Willis Geddis viewed himself as a man who could do no wrong. My father dubbed him 'the angel with whiskers.'

John Browning, called 'the going man', worked on and off for my grandfather for two years. He once spent his entire summer wages on an automobile, which in those days was looked upon as a foolish purchase. John was so frightened by the prospect of what Herb might think of him, he parked the car behind a tree down the lane. Herb saw the car and John quit rather than face Herb's criticism.

Les Newman lost his own farm during the depression and came to work for Herb in 1939. He was a very dependable and capable worker. Other people who were available to help out in times of need included retired farmers and down-on-their luck men who'd lost their own land and needed the work. Blake Farren was one such man. A regular in the local garage, the meeting place for the men who'd gather there to drink pop, eat peanuts, smoke, joke and tell stories, he was particularly fascinating to me because he recited long passages of poetry memorized from his own school days.

George Kemp was a hayseed lothario. He was a baggy-pant bucolic lady's man. He always had a girlfriend or a live-in woman. He was not handsome. He rarely bathed. He shaved but every few weeks. His trousers were held in place by twine. His shirts were soiled. And yet, he was a lover. A Don Juan of the wheat field. A Casanova of the threshing crew. When he wasn't working, I never saw him once without a lady on his arm. He had no teeth and when he laughed, a line of spittle followed like a thread from the beak of a nesting bird.

Tom and Blake and George were men I knew. I worked with them all. With Tom I'd shocked wheat, painted pails, polished halters, mucked out pens, ridden the stone boat, ridden the wagon, stooked bales, held halters snubbed for the ringing of bulls. We were always the ones to blame for the hogs who slipped past when we were loading pigs. We took the tongue lashings when bales tumbled down from loads or wagons jack-knifed on the grade. Never smart enough, tall enough, strong enough, quick enough, brave enough, dexterous enough, skilled enough, we were expected to stand and watch for hours while the barn tap ran to fill the trough. Whenever a hammer was needed we were sent running.

My favourite story of all the stories of hired help over the years is a story from the war years. My father's sister Stella told this story more than once and every time I heard it I was glad for the telling. There was a prisoner of war camp in nearby Chatham where they kept the German POW's. In the summer, they brought a few to our farm to work in the harvest under armed guard. With the arrival of dinner hour, they were brought indoors to the dining room, much like any regular thrashing crew. They sat around the table and were served by my grandmother and her daughters.

As Stella remembers it, they were just boys. At the time, my uncle was enlisted in the Canadian navy and serving on a destroyer escorting merchant ships across the Atlantic to Great Britain. It was perilous work. Many a ship went down to the wolf packs patrolling those waters. My grandmother had a photograph of her son in his naval uniform hung on the wall at the end of the table. In the photograph he was hugging his sister Stella and smiling in his uniform with his tallywhacker and his bell-bottoms and his bucket hat making it obvious that he was a man in the service of his country.

One young German prisoner of war lifted his fork and pointed at the photograph, asking my grandmother in broken English, "Is that your son?" When she replied, "Yes," he wept.

As a young boy hearing that story, I thought to myself, he is weeping for home, for his own mother, his own sister, perhaps his own wife. I decided then and there never to allow my nation to choose my enemies. These hired men. These German POWs could easily have been sighting through the periscope of a conning tower, taking aim on my grandmother's son.

If I think back on all the men who were hired to work our land, I feel the privilege of having known many and various lives at work. I think of my own generation. Of Stanley who came to work. He failed to pace himself so he was good for only one load before becoming sick as a dog. Of Whitey, the Nystagmus suffering albino who bragged of his sex life in Detroit and spent time in jail for robbing the local candy store. Of the boy with the unfashionably long hair who could not afford a hair cut. Of the neighbours who worked for us for a day. The men who came and went from table. The men who drank beer at noon on the porch and then returned to the field. The men who waited out the rain in the metallic thunder of the tin-roofed shed. The men who washed-up in the galvanized tub on the porch and ate three pieces of pie each. I think even of the days of the Depression when my father said, "A medical doctor who came here to work, said to my dad, 'Herb have you got some work for me?' And when my dad said, 'No, I'm sorry,' he cried, so dad gave him toil for the day in exchange for meals before he went on his way." In those hard times there were doctors, lawyers, professional men walking the roads and riding the rails. Uncle John recalls how the people in the city brought peanut butter jars, honey pails, anything they might carry to the fair barns to beg for milk.

One Boy's 4H Story

I TURNED TWELVE ON November 24th, 1963, two days after the assassination of John F. Kennedy. I marked my birthday with my family by watching the murder of Lee Harvey Oswald on live television. In February of the same season, the Beatles landed in New York. Like young people everywhere, I too was caught up in Beatlemania. I can still recall my Uncle John importuning me to come down stairs to watch the Beatles. "It's important," he said. I had never heard of them and thought perhaps they were puppets like Topo Gigio, Ed Sullivan's Italian puppet pal, who sat on his sleeve saying, "Eddie," to the amusement of no child I ever knew. In any event, I gave in and joined my family there in the parlour to watch the joyful, ebullient band from Liverpool, England. That experience changed my life. Even for children living in rural regions of Ontario, rock and roll music had become important. That was also the year I became eligible to belong to 4-H. I had been a member of the Tri-County Shorthorn Calf Club for two years and had been looking forward to joining 4-H ever since I could remember. I loved working with livestock, most especially cattle, so it seemed natural to join the 4-H Beef Calf Club, which I did that spring. I didn't really feel much like becoming a farmer, but our rural roots go deep in this province, and as one of my uncles liked to say, "most of the humus is in the roots."

The 4-H Beef Calf Club had its culmination in a show at Highgate Fair on Saturday of Thanksgiving weekend in October of 1964. At this fair I would be expected to show a calf in the calf class and in the showmanship class, where I would be given points for the presentation of my calf. In preparation for this show we met at the home of the leader or one of the members once a month, where we learned about animal husbandry, and planned projects for display at the local agricultural fairs. The leader would teach us about feeding, grooming and caring for our calves. As well as being a challenge, with many hours of hard work, it was great fun. I was a member in good standing of that club every subsequent year until my nineteenth birthday in 1970 and I was the club reporter for two years. In that capacity I was responsible for giving monthly reports on club activities to the local newspaper. It was my premier assignment as a writer and I felt quite proud seeing my byline in print.

My first 4-H calf was a high-strung, skittish, white, purebred Shorthorn heifer registered as Leeland Poppy the Eighth. A few days before her dam calved, I fell through the mow hole down eight feet of empty air into her pen. My cousin Billy and I had been clapping the pigeons on the mow floor. We were running end-to-end, looking up. I saw them as one might startled angels. Their wings beat in a white feathered flurry above me as I strode the void, my legs churning a vacuum as I fell. Fortunately the fall was broken by a rather-cushiony cowpat in a full fluff of new straw. Nonetheless, I had the wind knocked out of me, and the poor startled cattle beast worried over the half-door, mooing mournfully as if she thought she had dropped me as a cow might drop a calf.

My cousin Bill ran to the house to tell my mother I was dead. To this day, I wonder why it took her so long to get to the barn. I imagine her at the sink, washing the dishes as Bill bursts in. "Johnny's dead. Johnny's dead."

"What's that dear? Johnny's dead? Just let me finish these last few plates and we'll come see." And I see her drying her hands, folding the towel, calling my father, "George, come to the barn. It seems, Johnny's dead, or so Billy says." And my father, rattling his paper free of its wrinkles, folds the news, rises and comes to the kitchen.

"Just let me put on my shoes. I'll only be a moment. What's happened to him, then."

"He fell out of the mow."

"Again," my father might be saying.

"Yes, again." my mother replies.

"Do you mind if we come see, as well," say Uncle Hugh and Aunt Isabelle who are visiting at the time.

I think of them in their lack-worry, not because they don't care. Not because they don't love. But because this is the third occasion of my having plunged from a mow hole. I fell at my cousin Bill's farm and my head struck a salt block thus gashing my scalp and making it bleed profoundly. We went to the house my forehead beribboned, my tan cap stained, my topknot like the free flowing of a crimson party favour. We were joking as we came into the kitchen about how the salt would have instantly disinfected the wound. My Aunt Dorothy took one look at me, raced to the hand pump at her sink and began to prime the water, the rag she held in her left hand staying dry over the floor, as she rocked back and forth in worry. Even though the bleeding stopped eventually, my aunt decided I should be taken to the doctor in any event. Her son, my cousin Al, was sixteen. He was assigned the task of taking us to old Doc in their black Studebaker. It had been raining all day and as we slewed onto the road at the end of their lane, we caught marl and slid into the ditch. By the time we were hauled out, it was decided that I be taken home instead of to the doctor's. When my mother said I couldn't go to the movies that night with Al and Bill, I wept and she gave in. We went to the drive in and saw a film called, *Burn Witch Burn*, which for thirty years I referred to as *Witch Burn Witch*. All night Al and his friend passed a tobacco pipe back and forth, sharing the burning weed and then at midnight we arrived at a white line on a black road and I experienced my first drag race. That was the occasion of my first falling.

The second tumble I took was from the straw mow. I fell through the mow hole directly into the sow trough. It fit me like a metal coffin. I startled the hungry sow from her wet slop which splashed around me like a plaster maker's bad day. I counted myself lucky for that soft landing and I looked up to Tom's face looking down from mow-hole heaven like a face at a far window framed in straw.

In any event, this third drop seemed the hardest. I had the wind knocked out of me and perhaps that is why Bill thought me dead. By the time he descended the ladder and found me there and then raced to the house to report my untimely demise, I was lying on my back in brown cowpie unable to breathe. Perhaps as well, my sudden, unexpected and unannounced arrival from above might provide some explanation as to why the daughter that that cow bore two days later never really liked me, nor ever broke to the halter so I could show her in the calm way to which I had become accustomed with the other Poppy cow progeny.

A year later at the Tri-county show in July of 1964, the yearling calf, born get of the startled cow, dragged me around the fairgrounds racetrack as if I were a harrow meant to smooth the earth. At Dresden fair she bucked me down the cattle chute like a rodeo bull. Not to be outwitted, I tied her every day that summer, and groomed her as a mother might her favourite daughter. I bathed her, currycombed her flanks, teasled her tail switch, and fed her the most delicious rolled oats and molasses and nothing but the sweetest hay. Every month I weighed her and kept a record of her growth and progress by measuring her girth. In October, though she may have been the loveliest, most pampered calf at the fair, still her stubborn streak proved undefeated. In the 4-H show ring she flung her head, balked at the chain, stepped back, out of kilter, legs akimbo, a second after she'd been stood square, and generally showed me up for an incompetent and slightly frustrated fellow. Although she may have placed first in her class, she doomed me to the bottom for showmanship, which means I was docked points for the behaviour of the animal in the show ring. I'm quite certain that my own behaviour was less than exemplary by that point as well. However, years later, in September 1970, she became Supreme Champion of the show at London fair and earned my father the distinction of Supreme Breeder as well. In addition to being the dam to two subsequent calf-club calves, she was also to bring the best offer-to-buy that my father ever received for a cow in all his years as a herdsman.

As I said, my first year in 4-H was 1964, the year the world fell in love with four lads from Liverpool known as the Beatles. Everyone was affected in some way or another by the mania. Old men donned Beatle wigs to amuse themselves and to poke good-natured fun at our generation's musical heroes. Even 4-H got into the act. At the very first 4-H rally I attended, I have a vivid recollection of four leaders in bad wigs strumming kitchen brooms, beating out a fake rhythm on boxes with sawed-off sticks and lip syncing to one of the Fab Four's real rave-up numbers, "Twist and Shout". Those fellows shook their hair and waggled their hips to our great delight. I was thrilled to think that I belonged to such a cool organization. I may have lived in the country, but I was part of the larger world.

When I was sixteen I became a member of the Ridgetown 4-H Sheep Club. Given my life in a family of shepherds, my experience in the 4-H Sheep Club should have been one of distinction. With one possible exception, I was certainly the most experienced shepherd in the club. However, although I am grateful to have been involved, my two clearest remembrances are still mortifying to think back on. I recall going completely mute at one meeting where we were expected to place a class of Shropshire lambs and then justify our choices with a brief talk. I stood there shuffling, looking down at my feet and breaking into a cold sweat. Suddenly I knew nothing whatsoever about sheep. The silence seemed eternal. I don't recall saying anything. I remember thinking that everyone expected me to be an expert. How could I say anything without spoiling my own unearned and undeserved reputation? Better to stay mum and let them think it was merely a matter of stage fright. Fortunately, the leader sympathized with my plight and moved on the next lad. In no small part, due to that simple act of kindness, along with further judging experience at those meetings, I was able to redeem myself later on by winning first place over all in the Kent County Annual Livestock Judging Competition in 1969. At that event we had to place classes of steers, heifers, lambs, and market hogs, and then to speak to a large gathering about why we had made our choices. I am still quite proud of my accomplishment, having proven my ability to make important choices and speak in front of a crowd. The trophy marking that occasion sits on a shelf in my study festooned with writing awards. As I write this, I can glance to the figure of a bronzed sheep framed in laurels raised on a wooden plinth. From the base I have draped a Souwesto words medallion, and Austin International Poetry Festival 'poet of 2000' badge, and three Milton Acorn People's Poetry Award medallions. Here the bucolic meets the literary.

The second humiliating event of my short career in the 4-H Sheep Club involved the annual show at Ridgetown fair in early August. We had each raised one wether and one ewe lamb for the show. The show ring was surrounded by bleachers and there were about thirty people watching our progress. I brought my lamb out for the ewe class and found myself overlooked, even though I was being frequently looked over. The judge placed all the other lambs in the class except for mine. He kept coming back to me and then walking away looking perplexed. I was thinking either he was going to cull me from the class, or he was going to make a special case for the excellence of my lamb as an exemplary of the breed. After all, I had grown accustomed to prize ribbons. My grandfather was quoted in the paper as he noted the fact that he had sacks and sacks of first prize ribbons in the barn. Our den was full of silver platters, bronze plaques, sterling trophies and photographs of supreme champion flocks of the show. The cabinet was full from top to bottom with evidence of excellence. And I was next in line. Finally, after much hesitation, the judge strolled sheepishly in my direction, bent close and whispered, "Uh, John, you do know this is a ewe lamb class, don't you?" It was only then that I noticed his black wig, his pencilled-on eyebrows, his completely beardless face, his denuded arms. That was small consolation for my humiliation. In a flash I knew what this depilated man meant by his indecisive actions. He was seeking the kindest way of letting me know I'd brought a wether out instead of a ewe. In front of all these people, I had to take my wether back into the barn and bring out my ewe lamb. Here I was, the descendant of five generations of established shepherds, having grown up on a farm where sheep had been an integral part of the life on the land for close to one hundred years, and I could not even sex the breed. Needless to say, my cheeks were hot with shame, but I finished the task at hand. The afflicted judge had been very kind and considerate. Quickly, and with confidence, he placed my lamb second in a class of ten. Next, I showed my wether, having survived the scrutiny of the hairless judge and one of the greatest embarrassments of my life.

I graduated from high school; spent my last year at home as a member of Junior Farmers; attended the University of Western Ontario where I acquired three degrees, including a Master of Arts in Teaching English; became a teacher of Secondary School English for fourteen years and have since gone on to a full-time career in writing.

My mother and uncle are still on the land. Perhaps they are disappointed that I left home. I may not have chosen a career in agriculture, nor a life in the country, but agriculture has played an important role in forming my values and in defining my concerns. And although being a member of 4-H didn't keep me from leaving for a life as a professional writer in the city, it did provide me with much learning and companionship through the troubled years of adolescence in the 60's.

I visit the farm frequently and always enjoy seeing how the sheep are doing, though now the sheep are all gone. Uncle John finally sold the last of the flock south of the border. My last recollection of the sheep at home involved my father and my writer friend Roger Bell. Dad handed me a ram and said, "hold that ram while I show Roger something." I gripped him firmly by the chops wool and he stood steady and calm in my grasp. Roger mentioned later that he was impressed by how I eased into old habits. He praised me for the way the ram seemed instantly to know he was being held by someone who knew exactly how to hold a sheep. I was comforted and flattered by his words. I have a clear recall of feeling the jaw line of that final buck under the heel of my hand. I could feel how instantly calm he was, how much a part of me knew exactly what was needed.

When my own boys were little city lads, my dad always provided them with an opportunity to show sheep in an open class at Alvingston Fair. The normally calm sheep would instantly begin to hop about and pull away and drag themselves loose and run along the fence-line of the fair pens. They knew the neophyte in my boys. They recognized the lack of knowledge in their too tight or overly-feckless grasp. One generation of being away, and all was lost to them. What I could do at age five, they could not do at twelve. I could see myself as a five-year-old boy calming a ton-heavy herd bull with no more than the tug of my pinky finger in his nose ring. And there we were at the fair with my father not understanding why his grandsons could not even handle a gentle ewe.

And yet, I still get a thrill when I go to small fairs and see the young people grooming their calves or talcing their hogs. My cousin Bill had been a member of the 4-H Market Hog Club, and I can't look at those clean pigs without giving a slight smile, remembering him with his cane and his hog, meandering in the ring, with all those pigs desperate for escape, exploring each other and every possible exit with their snouts. And the smells of fresh straw, good hay, sweet molasses and rolled oats, hair spray, saddle soap, shoe blacking, linseed oil, brasso, creosote, rich manure of grain-fed, show-fitted beasts, and even the slight lime smell of fresh whitewash on the walls of a 4-H barn, can excite a memory of a special time when I too was a teenager. With my whole life in front of me, I remember grooming my calf or plucking straw and washing the dock wool of my lamb, hoping to take first prize, not motivated by the idea of defeating my friends, but to prove that I had accomplished something special. And as I remember each calf, and as I recall every lamb, I also carry with me a fond memory of my club mates and leaders. Glenn Wooton, one of my two 4-H Calf Club leaders came to a poetry reading I gave to help launch a new book store in my home town of Ridgetown. He knows how thrilled I was that he took the time to come out. Perhaps he came to see what had become of the lad he'd known back then, when I was a slightly shy boy with much to learn.

That boy with much to learn is now a man. When he stood with his friend Don Linehan upon the dock of a fishing port in Lunenburg, Nova Scotia, looking out to sea where a fish trawler was being followed by gulls swooping down and touching into the waves to feed in the wake of that boat's passage, he remembered how, while he was springtoothing a field, the gulls would land in the damp earth behind him to feed on the worms and grubs he'd turned. He glanced at his friend and told him this story which seemed to connect the land and the sea and thereby the life of the farmer to the life of the fisherman. And these two, both being poets, knew in that instant that they'd been given a gift. They knew that for anyone who had a head to learn, a heart to feel, and a hand to turn the soil or touch the water, there is this truth, "Everything comes from the earth." We are all guardians of that trust and he who plays some small role in promoting and preserving that trust is doing important work, good work, work that honours our dust.

Driving Like a Farmer

WHEN YOU GROW up on a farm, you learn how to drive the minute you can reach the pedals. That doesn't mean necessarily that you drive well, especially when it comes to the proximity of crops.

My grandfather, Herb Lee, for his part, drove only the E.M.F., a car famous for stalling when it was stopped. I was told by my uncle that he caught his father in the implement shed filing the points with a horse rasp. Someone else told me that he'd seen Herb drive to the village, passing his wife on the road on the way. And later, coming home, he passed her again with their children in tow, toting bags full of groceries. Even then Herb breezed by and into the lane to the farm. Either he didn't see why they needed a ride, or as an elderly friend said, "Maybe Herb didn't think he could get that car going again once he'd stopped." I think of him putt putting along like Toad of Toad Hall, oblivious to his poor wife.

For our own part, my sister and I walked the mile to and from school every day, rain or shine, March wind or sleet and snow. And I still recall being passed by our dad in the truck on his way to the mill, the seat, vacant beside him as he breezed past.

The first occasion of finding myself behind the wheel of an automobile, my sister and I were two tiny kids lost behind the dash of our dad's green Dodge. He'd left the keys in the ignition and we were pretending to drive, when the car suddenly fired up and went drifting slowly in reverse. My sister opened the door and leapt out leaving me to steer that slow machine as it humped to a stop on the harrows which flattened two tires with a hiss and a sigh as it settled like a wagon in mud.

I finally learned to drive at around age ten. I rode the clutch lurching across hay stubble in the farm pickup under the tutelage of my less-than-patient uncle. That old pickup bucked and jumped like a horse in the barn all winter. I stopped and stalled, stopped and stalled under my uncle's glare. "Let out the clutch easy, boy! Easy!" Eventually, I overcame all difficulty, circling groundhog holes and leaving behind a crush of stubble like two men walking.

The first time I ever drove on the road, I was twelve. "Get in behind the wheel and drive that truck to the mill, boy," my uncle said, sliding into the suicide seat beside me. I can still almost feel first speed as I drove in first gear half-way to the village without shifting, the engine roaring, the transmission wanting to jump its cogs. I'd never shifted into a higher gear and I found that grind of going only after my uncle lashed me with his tongue, as we drifted loudly into neutral and from there into metal cog-mesh with a terrible noise, as if I were grinding wet corn. Eventually, I smoothed the final mile in second gear, fearing third. Needless to say, I didn't get to drive home. However, I can still see myself mounting the scales beside the wheat dust of the mill door with its beastly roar of grain becoming chop.

The premier occasion of ever driving alone on the road, arrived the day my father told me to hook on our cousin's little borrowed auger wagon and draw it the five miles home. I felt grown up at twelve, riding the hard seat with its sheepskin seat cover as I went purring down the lane and onto the country pavement, vacant for miles in two directions.

I knew things could go wrong even for full-grown men. I knew the story of our hired man who had dragged a wheel-locked manure spreader up and down the field, wearing ruts in his path deep as the run-off from heavy rains. The beaters were seized in tough dung and he just didn't look round. He simply drove back and forth, back and forth wondering why his load stayed heavy.

The same man also took a sharp turn too fast and too hard so his wheat jag tipped, the wagon spilling its burden into the deep ditch. He'd splintered the wagon tongue like a twisted board. And he never drove that tractor again for thirty years, cursing the damned thing for being wrongly made.

My uncle who taught me to drive had once come through the barnyard gate in high gear, coming so fast that he caught the post on his wheel and reefed it out of the earth like a high wind. I'd seen my dad stuck to the tractor axles, the engine housing slogged down in the mud like a sow in a wallow all day. I'd heard how some of my father's friends had missed the lane in the dark and driven right into the middle of the low front fields.

But I was a boy, and what men sometimes forgive in themselves or in one another, they won't allow in a youth. So, I knew I had something to prove. If I could do this thing without incident, then I would make my father as proud of me as he was of my cousin Stuart who'd been driving on the road since he was seven.

Everything about the day was beautiful. We had entered the halcyon hours of summer. The grain was in, the hardest work behind us, and I was looking forward to the first fairs of late July and early August. The sky above was blue as a Dutchman's shirt, the sun was high in the heavens, the air was thick and redolent with the perfume of drying second cut with only the haying to do. I raced along the road in that gasoline wind, the cicadas whining about me like high tension wires running the length of the world.

I didn't slow down for the straight miles. I hardly slowed down for the turns. But when I didn't slow down for the railway tracks, the tractor went bumpity-bump so the power-drive to the disengaged auger of the wagon came off the drawbar, thus stranding the thing on the rails in the path of a phantom train. "Surely," I prayed, "God wouldn't schedule a train for right now, not while I'm here with my heart in my brain like a hammer fixing a spike in a knot on a beam." I pulled to the side of the road and looked back with a lump in my throat like a half-swallowed pit of a peach gulped hard.

I was backing up to the tongue, when I heard the whistle from a mile away to the west. I instantly knew that I didn't have time to hook on. And like a foolish child, I'd rather have died than have failed. How might I explain to my father that a cow catcher gathered up metal and tossed it away in a crush like a soda pop can in the ditch to the side of the tracks.

Perhaps I was foolish, but I wasn't dumb. I turned the tractor around and nosed the wagon backwards out of danger, the tractor tread of my hind wheels feeling the whoosh and the shudder of a rushing wind as the diesel whistled past.

I didn't tell my father for another thirty years. My father, who once accidentally dropped the hydraulic of the farm disk and grooved macadam for a quarter mile, my father, who fell off the tractor riding the draw bar while his brother drove so he broke his pride and didn't walk well all winter that year. I couldn't tell that man this story. Not then. Not when I wanted his approval.

One of the recent times I was home, I turned right at the village and found myself following a brand spanking new pickup truck that pulled out in front of me, then straddled the centre line for the next half mile before taking the lane on the left like the English abroad.

"Look at that man," I said to my sons in the back seat. "He drives like a farmer," I said. "He thinks he owns the road because he's close to home," I said, meaning it all as a sort of a joke with a lesson inside. And then the truck stopped and my father got out for the mail at the road.

I laughed to know it was he. "What's the hurry?" I could almost hear him saying. "What do you make of the poor catch of hay? What do you think of the wheat still green? Did you notice the weeds in the beans?"

to measure my life
by the death of dogs

THE FIRST DOG of my five-dog life thus far was easily the best and brightest. Tippy was a beautiful blond-furred English collie mutt. A nine-week-old pup, he came to our farm when I was ten years old. He wagged half himself to greet me and climbed me to the ears and lapped my face with all the inner enthusiasm of thirst for spilled milk.

I have in my possession a favourite photograph from that first day. Boy and dog, we both almost broke for joy.

And he was clever. We had to put him in his pen when we worked in the garden, for he loved to hoe. We'd be there weeding the vegetables with the half-bored chop chop chop of the steel-faced hoe, and there he'd appear out of nowhere beside us, digging away, earth flying behind him in a brown fan. But sad to tell, he was still a dog who did not know the difference between wild carrot and the real. He could not distinguish thistle from aster, spud from nut grass. Out he'd haul the tomato vine so it flew in his jaw like a slightly acid-flavoured garden lamp. Into the pen he'd have to go.

I remember my mother harvesting a squash or two for supper, when he came up behind her trailing an entire gourd vine for the house.

A favourite tale of his undeniable intelligence involves a day when my mother, my sister, and I were out in the front yard playing badminton.

Anyone who has ever attempted that game out of doors knows that it inevitably leads to a quarrel. Any wind, any slightest breeze will have its way with the flight of the feathered shuttlecock. Barely touch the birdie and it sings into your opponent's forehead like a snub-nosed dart. Return it with whatever force you will; it rises, catches in a gust and lands behind your shoulder on the lawn like a shot bird.

So it went the day we three were playing a sprightly, though one-sided wind-favoured game until my sister, growing peevish, sassed my mother who decided to punish her with a willow switch across the calves to make her behave. Just a tiny swish across her bare legs to make her mind her tongue.

I can tell you, I was looking forward to that.

My mother crossed the yard to the weeping willow, snapped off a single catkin for weapon and moved menacingly in the direction of her daughter, my doomed sister. Oh the delicious anticipation. The almost palpable thrill.

The dog, seeing my mother in motion, ran to the very same tree, leapt into the wind, tore off a horse tail of branches and came trailing the swish across the grass.

My mother saw, stopped in her tracks and burst out laughing. The dog ran in victory circles. His mouth brooming the green.

My sister went unpunished (a great disappointment to me to this very day) and Tippy ran around and around trailing willow wand as if he'd swallowed a small horse tail-last and laughing as dogs laugh.

As I say, that dog was the most intelligent dog I have ever known save for one major flaw. He loved to chase vehicles. Cars. Buses. Trucks. Tractors. And as if that weren't perilous enough, he was not satisfied to chase them from behind. Nor did it give him pleasure to chase them from the side. He chose perversely to chase them from the front.

That was actually quite possible and relatively safe on our farm. The once or twice he managed to chase the odd school bus, he seemed to learn from the peril of road-work as bus bumpers sent him sprawling off into the ditch like flung mud.

Our barns are built on a hill at the top of a long farm lane. Halfway up the hill a large gate sits closed against intrusion and the loss of sheep to the road. Situated on either side of the lane are two sheep meadows with gates flung wide. Cars turning into the lane are forced to stop and open the lane gate. The sheep, grazing in the eastern pasture, upon hearing the engine of the car at the gate, would lift their heads from grazing, listen a heartbeat, turn together as blown cloud cluster turns, and run west towards the open gate like bad weather gathering at the head of the field.

Just as the car arrived at the top of the lane, the sheep would cross in a single trailing flock, thereby forcing the car to stop and let them pass to the very last straggle of moving wool, thus giving Tippy a perfect opportunity to run back and forth, back and forth in front of the vehicle, nipping at the chrome and making the cautious driver ease ahead ever so slowly toward the house with the scissor sound of teeth on shiny metal for company for fear of killing a sheep or crushing the dog.

Every once in a while that happy caution saved the life of a rogue ram or disgruntled ewe. I've seen one old dam lie down, sawing her cud, staying put like a landlady owed the rent.

The only occasion I ever crashed my motorcycle was when I was side-swiped by a darting wether late to cross.

What you must know about sheep in order to understand them, is their need to be together. If you have one sheep on one side of a fence and a hundred sheep on the other, by the end of an hour, either all the sheep will join the one, or the one will join the all. Thus it is that a bellwether works. So too, with a slaughterhouse Judas goat.

Whenever the guest of our farm would turn on the engine to leave, the sheep, as if perverse, would hear, raise their noses from the grass, listen intently and begin to run in their effort for egress, departing from the far corner of the west pasture, arriving at the hilltop just as the departing vehicle also arrived, thereby forcing a halt and giving good-dog Tippy a further opportunity to run back and forth, back and forth, nipping at the guilty chrome.

I wonder if in his mind he weren't creating a safety zone like some canine crossing guard.

I do not know, but I saw this ritual repeated hundreds if not thousands of times, unfolding as it should, safely for all concerned.

Then one awful day, the sheep were locked in the barn when a gasoline delivery truck made its way up the lane and to the tank. As it left, it struck the dog, snapping his spine like a green stick and hurling him branch-broken into the ditch at the side of the lane. Tom, the hired man, went down the lane, gathered up the crippled ruin in his arms, and carried the broken burden of our dog up the lane to where he handed him over to me. I could tell how he was bent wrong behind the front shoulders leaving his hind legs in a weird kicked-sideways L. I knew he would never walk again, if he did indeed survive.

I accepted the ruined dog from Tom and carried him up to where I set him in his dog pen in the dirt behind the ledge and then closed the door on darkness.

I begged my father to get the vet to either cure him or put him out of his misery. But that is not the way it goes on a working farm. We doctored our own livestock and the vet was called out at great expense only in the event of an emergency beyond our expertise. A breeched calf. A scoured lamb. Not a distempered cat or car-struck dog. These would either survive or perish.

And so I went to see Tippy, lying broken in his pen, lifting his head to lap a little water, and waiting it seemed to die. After a few days watching him languish and fail, I decided to act.

As he couldn't cross the threshold of the pen because of the height of the ledge, I decided to lift him out and set him down beyond the door.

I can still recall the exact look of the lawn. It was late autumn, early November, the grass still slightly green. First snow had just fallen, dusting the grass like icing sugar. It was the sort of snow whereon you leave green footprints wherever you go in the glaze.

I set the dog down in the day and he came alive with joy. He ran in circles of swath, dragging his hind legs like a sled. His mouth opened, his tongue lolled, and he laughed the way dogs laugh, with that silent, big-mouthed laughter of dogs. I clapped my hands and he ran and ran like a broken-winged bird.

He was the happiest creature I have ever witnessed to this very day.

Over the next few weeks, he learned how to run and he'd run so fast his hind end flew in the air like a flag. He ran on his front two legs, head down, neck turned so he could see where he was going.

If you'd come to our farm in those days, you'd have seen that dog chasing the cattle, herding the hogs, picking up speed even to climb the low end of the straw stack.

And then one night late in the winter, he died. Tom found him in February, frozen to the barn floor.

It breaks my heart still to think of that spirited collie with his deep and undefeatable joy in life, dying alone in the cold.

In the spring, at first thaw, we dug a hole and buried him along with other winter dead: a sow, a heifer, a few doomed runts, a bag of cut twine and Tippy set on top.

The next dog we called Wacky. He was whelped by the same bitch, but his was a dumb love. Then came Lady, named for Lady Diana by my mother. Lady was a wet little hospital mop of a thing. All timid flop of hair and barely there. Not much of a farm dog, but mother loved her.

The last farm dog just up and died a few weeks ago. They found her lying stiff behind the truck. My father called her, 'retarded'. A dog should be smarter than the owner, he said. That dog had been a Boo Radley dog who'd only be seen when the neighbour dog came over to visit. Otherwise, she'd hidden in the barn under a pile of bags, or in the implement shed under the baler. She'd spend all her energy hiding. I told Dad to put all his valuables in the black hole behind the dog's nest. That's the only place she guards with her two dark eyes shining out from the deep recesses of her nest.

As for me, I've lived longer away from the farm than on the farm. I've had my share of dogs. Ebenezer, 'heavy sneezer' I'd had for eighteen years. He learned two tricks. One was to yawn and the other to sneeze. Since he died, we've had our Sydney. Food-smart dog that she is, she doesn't do anything that most dogs do. Though born a spaniel, she can't even swim. One time she fell in the pool and sank like a stone. The boys had to dive in and rescue her from the bottom at the deep end where she stood like a garden statue fallen in. We love her, but I suppose there's no love for a dog as dear or which runs so deep as the love of a child for the first dog of his boyhood.

I look at that photograph snapped that first day of our greeting, the day that a beautiful collie pup climbed my lap and licked my face for love and all the joy and glory of a sea that breaks upon a stone.

Attacked by All the Animals

AT MY FATHER'S funeral my uncle remembered me as boy, "You were trapped in the barn, shouting, 'Help! Help! Save me! Save me!' A ram stood between you and the doorway and would not let you out." Thus it was with me and the livestock. Though I loved the dumb domestic beasts on our farm with all my heart, more often than not that love went unrequited.

Our farm was a farm of livestock more than cash crop. My grandfather once told my father, "what walks off this land pays for this land." By that he was strongly suggesting that the material benefit of the beast far outstripped that of the plant. And so, I grew up amongst animals. By the age of first consciousness, I had seen more of sex, birth and death than most would experience in many lifetimes. I had seen bulls standing cows, boars mounting sows, rams covering ewes, cocks breeding hens, toms taking felines on feed sacks, felines in gutters, felines in wild, snarling, thrashing, spinning, coupling barn ruts more like fighting than loving.

And I had been present at midnight rituals of spring lambing in barn light, my uncle stripped to the waist in the chill to give the ewe comfort and see her safely through twins, their wool a slight crimson yellow with offal the colour of Mercurochrome or iodine swabbed in bloody cotton.

I have turned the dew claw of a knuckled under half-born breeched calf or set newborn piglets in heat lamps that lit the farrowing straw bright pink like an Easter basket's decorative shredded paper.

And I had seen death and decay up close. I had helped kill hogs hung by the hocks from the apple branch. I had held down wethers while my uncle spilled their lives to the earth. I had culled runts and ended the lives of crush-skulled cats. I had watched scoured calves lose the light, their eyes gone glassy as brown ice. I'd watched distempered generations of kittens sneeze and pass. I'd seen thin runts starve and fade over days among their strong and greedy siblings. I'd seen ewes upside down in ditches, and cows scorched to the horns by lightning.

We had a dozen species and quite a few breeds of most domestic farm stock. We had a proud plough horse named Prince. As a boy I'd ridden high on his sweating shoulders, working the garden near enough the orchard that I could reach up and touch passing branches of peach blossom and buds of snow apple. He was a solitary holdover from the days of a working team. We also had a fair pony two winters in our keeping. We had mostly purebred, shorthorn beef cattle, though we also owned two gentle jerseys kept for milk and for butter in the house. And we had one wild-eyed black Galloway cow bought for the merit of her calves. We had purebred, longwool, Lincoln, good-land sheep, the pride of the farm, first brought over from the old country by my great-grandfather in 1889. We had a dozen or more laying hens, a brood of Muscovy ducks, a single collie dog, and at one point I had husbanded a population of thirteen adult barn cats. The generations of their kittens came and went, going invisibly after rats under corn cribs and after mice in the fields and mows. We had all that, and yet, though I loved working with the livestock, I was attacked by virtually every animal of every species and every breed and kind save dogs over the course of my time at home.

I was attacked by a sheep. Though most people are not aware of the dangers of sheep, they can be quite perilous with your back turned. I was struck from behind by a cross, black-faced Suffolk ram at my maternal grandfather's farm when I was six. That buck caught me running and butted me so I flew from his top knot right over a five-foot board fence. I was also attacked by my grandfather's gander that very same visit. He came hissing at me out of nowhere and chased me from the farmyard to the sanctuary of the little root cellar just beside the house. He pecked and beat his wings at the door like a storm branch in a high wind.

As for sheep, even my Uncle John, a career shepherd, was knocked silly by a prize ram. One day, when he wasn't on his guard, he was bent over, his head only inches from the manger, and this particularly rambunctious buck saw his broad-beamed brown khaki buttock and simply came hard-headed to the task. Bang, and he knocked my doubled-over uncle head first into the manger, thus stunning him silly as he hit the board with his skull like a ram in rut and afterwards nursed a single first prize crimson ribbon of blood trickling down to prove himself dumb.

I was not exactly attacked by horses, though I had heard of horses taking thumbs like carrots or sugar sticks. At Norfolk Fair one year, a quarter horse mistook a boy's thatch of dyed-green hair for a twitch of grass and grazed him half bald on top. Though I was never bitten by horses, I have been stood upon by our Percheron plough horse Prince. I was holding his harness when he took a misstep and found my shoe pinching my toes in my runners flat as pounded dough. And he was dumb-legged as a pillar under a barn beam. However much I struck him for the pain, he simply stood there crushing, till I managed to slip my foot flat as paper, my flat toes squirting out, smarting and throbbing like sledge blows in my blood. I'm not certain he ever even knew what he'd done to me in my runners. He just moved his feathered front foot and planted his leg like a fourth oak on the ground. I was but a mere mouse to stamp.

The pony we kept for two winters was a different matter altogether. Ponies are usually much smarter than horses and like most small breeds are often quite mean. My maternal grandfather loved horses. After he retired from farming, he kept ponies in his barn on the edge of a field on the outskirts of the town. One particular spotted Shetland named Champ hated children. Only my cousin Stuart could ride him with ease. The rest of us he bucked clean off the saddle.

A favourite trick of his was to pin back his ears and run full out for the apples. One particular low branch would rake us clean and send us flying in a shudder of blossoms. Thus we learned gravity. Thus we learned the lesson of riding Champ. Hold him up with authority so the bit made him chew metal like hard green pears. Otherwise you became a mere nuisance like a fly bite on his back.

The pony we kept over winter on our own farm belonged to a man named Tiny. Tiny farmed out each of his four ponies, one each to willing keepers in the country. We kept our pony fat and warm in a barn stall for our riding pleasure. This pony spent his summers and the autumn walking a wheel for money, plodding fair fallow with village children in his saddle. Bored and lazy with life, longing for freedom and leisure, he was like most ponies, cruel by nature. A slave to the whip and the wheel, he came to our farm for the luxury of good hay, clean straw, and for a treat, brothy oats in warm water. But after the thrill and novelty of riding, we soon left him mostly in the misery and solitude of his barn stall growing lonely and nervous with the need for exercise.

One particular village brat used to come up to the farm after school to take our pony out of his pen. When we watched that lad, he'd simply strap on the saddle and go for a short ride. The pony was balky and skittish under his weight. One time I saw the pony take off and slide on a patch of ice sending this punk flying like a flung grain sack. He landed wincing and swearing on hard ground. He grabbed the reins and shook the bit in the pony's mouth till it rattled foam. What we didn't know was that when we weren't there watching, that village lad had been tying him up to a fence and beating him till he was wild and angry. If we'd known that, we probably would have cheered the drama of seeing him in flight from the saddle.

On one occasion, I remember, after a long period of having left the pony alone in the barn unridden for weeks, I took him out, saddled him and attempted to ride him around the yard. The second I was in saddle, he pinned back his ears, bucked me off and ran full out for the sheep pasture. I can still see him in my mind's eye, racing, ears pinned, tail out straight, neck stretched, belly low as grass, coursing the fence in a blur of nose, mane, withers and tail, girth brushing ground like a ditch dog after cars. He ran for freedom, ran for cruelty and pain, ran for tedium and loneliness, and though I was sore from the fall, I knew he deserved better than I, better also than that boy from the village with his cruel whip, far better than solitude and our dark stall. He deserved this. To run full out and away from the walk wheel of the fairgrounds, away from the clip clop under town kids, away from his man Tiny, here in this winter field, pushing his limits, feeling the wind in his lungs for all the life that was in him.

Though he never actually attacked me, he did make me sorrow for my own cruel husbanding over those two privileged winters I'd known him.

And I was attacked by cows. For the most part, our cattle were calm, docile, and compliant. But we had a few that were cross in calving. We had one particular cow my father called "the Carr cow." The Carr cow he named because he'd bought her from a man named John Carr who lived on the old Talbot estate near St. Thomas, Ontario.

Most of our horned cattle had either trimmed stubs, or horns curved decoratively forward in beautiful half-circles groomed that way by the wearing of horn weights. But the Carr cows were mature by the time of purchase and they had been left to nature. Their atavistic horns grew out and straight up like sharp-ended heliotropes pricked at the sun. Thus they were perfect weapons for goring. If a Carr cow ran at you, you got out of the way.

There was one occasion when two of my cousins, my sister and I were out walking across the cattle yard. For whatever reason, our dog started chasing the Carr cow's calf. Instead of taking exception to the dog's business, that cow came trotting at us, racing our way, head down, horns razoring out. I don't know how we accomplished it, but all four of us crossed a fatal distance, leapt the fence, and floated up the corn crib to the very topmost wire before that cross cow hit the wire below us full tilt sending a shudder through the posts in both directions like a softly radiant explosion in a blown stump. That fence wowed against her top poll and sent her hurtling backward. Just a little stunned, she loped the fenceline looking up to where we were, high up on the grid in the red snow fence of the corn crib. If she could have climbed, she would have climbed.

As for the dog, he grew bored with calf play and simply ran off after adventure while the Carr cow's calf joined its mother and they left together. As for the four of us, we waited an hour in the rotten-yellow heights of harvested field corn till we could be certain of our safety.

Another time, I was driving the cattle back the lane to the pasture. I hadn't noticed her calf behind me until the Carr cow took exception and turned her horns against me. She bellowed once and charged. I turned to run away when she caught me. She hooked one horn under one arm, one horn under the other and she flipped me on her forehead so I was lifted right out of my tied-up running shoes which I left behind me in the dust as I came down hard behind her. Her calf caught up and passed me and she left me there broken of breath in a stunned heap, grateful to be alive.

I was never attacked by bulls, though I'd been pinned by their bellows behind doors. The worst bull attack I'd ever heard about involved a tame Hereford herd bull owned by an acquaintance of my father's. That man had been walking in the cow pasture when the herd bull was out with the cows while the cows were in heat. The bull was tame as a lap dog. The man could walk up and place his own forehead between those broad, curved horns and lean in close as if to think a shared thought. But that day was different. The farmer knew he was in trouble when he caught the wild look in the bull's eyes a second too late. The bull came at him and caught him in the fleshy love handles, lacing the man's ample gut with a red horn. He gored him to the ground and pushed him across the pasture on his knees. Fortunately, the farmer had left his combine in the open and he managed to crawl underneath and secure himself behind a wheel. The bull bellowed, backed up, charged and struck, charged and struck, sending an angry shudder through the whole machine. The man lay there helpless and bleeding until someone saw his plight while passing on the road. He rescued him from his peril and the usually-tame bull simply went trotting back to his harem. The man did not blame the bull. Neither did he sell him. Rather he put the lesson to nature as a warning against ever making a pet from a bull again.

We had a boar who ran with the sows. Unlike cattle, pigs are able to bite. Boars have tusks that can rip you open like a party favour. We owned long-nosed, floppy-eared Landrace sows, and a few long-snouted rusty-brown Tamworths. But we had one cross, razor-tusked Yorkshire boar. You had to carry a sawed-off hockey stick with you wherever you went in the yard, because he'd attack you if you weren't so armed. Even then, he might take a chance and run at you whenever the sows were in heat. You'd have to give him one good solid wack across the snout so his teeth buzzed regret. That would be enough to warn him off and send his boar stink running.

As for the sows, I feared them even more than the boar because it was necessary to get in the pen with them when they were protecting their piglets from harm. You might slop them over the pen boards when they were hungry and grunting to have you there. You might water them from a safe vantage, spilling the slop on their foreheads and down their long noses. You might fling the parings and apple swill and hurl the corn cobs like broken-winged birds. But it was absolutely necessary to get in the pen with those thousand pound mothers in order to snip the black teeth from the piglets, or castrate their sons, or check on the health of their runts.

I hated doing any of the aforementioned tasks because the sows would come at you, their jaws snapping, their mouths foaming, their jowls shakings, their grunts full-bellied and fearfully threatening harm. They'd bite at your boots and chomp at your shirt. I'd been told that when pigs bite they can't let go, their jaws lock and they'll have what they're biting whether it be finger or thumb, calf sinew or face. More than once I've leapt the boards to escape, my uncle laughing and ridiculing me for my cowardice. And though I was never actually hurt by a sow, I still fear them and I still hear their loud huffs and snorts as they came at me, their voices full of slobber and groan, their bodies smelling like the sour essence of cut rhubarb.

I can still remember my father and I kneeling in the farrowing pen, catching the little boars by the leg, and after castration, releasing the cut barrows. As my father said, "a barrow is a gentleman who has lost his standing in the community in which he resides." My Dad used a razor blade, made a quick incision in the scrotum, pinched out each small blue-black testicle, sliced its vesicles, and tossed it over his shoulder. The sow who had till then been snorting and threatening and chomping her jaws on pant legs would turn and chase and gobble up the little delicacy as if he were tossing away only the best blue-black sweet candy.

We'd dust the bloody sack with disinfectant, then let loose the only-recently-neutered piglet who would race away into circles of happy straw, celebrating his freedom as if he'd simply gotten away with mischief.

The only time I ever suffered an injury at this task was on the occasion when my father accidentally cut the tip of my finger. That wound bled brightly and was contaminated by the pools of pig spoor near our work. Over the next several hours it swelled up and turned a livid purple. I spent one night suffering the most painful throbbing I can ever recall. My mother took me black handed to the doctor who lanced the injury and gave me antibiotics. I suppose it must have been blood poisoning. To this day I have yet to feel such pain.

Despite my kindness and good will, I have been attacked by barn kittens. Born wild in the straw mow, they needed to be tamed like ferals. I was a patient and a loving master. I learned to wait them out and find their comfort. Once too often I've heard the hiss and felt the needle prick of angry claws from reaching prematurely into dark nests. I learned to tantalize those clowders with fly-drowning pie plates of cow's milk. I'd wait patiently for hours until they came hungry to the lip of tin. They'd lap and leave, lap and leave, watching me all the while until they'd grown accustomed to my presence. Eventually, they'd lap and stay, lap and stay until the slightly cream-yellow fly float disappeared into a blink. Thus I've tamed a dozen generations. Thus I've become their favourite. Thus I became master of an all-boys choir of hungry toms. Thus I conducted singing kittens and calico mothers mewing with kittens clutched in their mouths like mending. And so, no cats attacked me for the last few years of my stay on the farm, though the barn cats soon disappeared with my leaving.

The worst animal attack I suffered occurred the day I was attacked by a duck. We had about seven ducks we raised for eating. They were good fly catchers and they free-ranged between the house and barn keeping down the pests. A duck can eat its own weight in flies every day, and Lord knows, pigs can nurture flies. I've been in the pig barn when you could scoop up a handful of flies like a buzzing fist full of insect buckwheat. The drake of the flock was very cross and very territorial. I've heard that some people keep watch geese instead of watch dogs. Water fowl can be extremely aggressive. I had a fifteen-year-old ancestor crippled by a swan when his father was grounds keeper at Mallow Castle in nineteenth century Ireland. He eventually died from his injuries. You could say I had an ancestor killed by a swan and not be a liar.

So, it's no wonder that when I was five years old I was attacked by a duck. I was walking from barn to house when I must have come too close the flock. He flew up and landed on my head, dug his toe claws into my scalp and flacked his wings like a hurry-up angel fanning against the side of my face. I must have been quite a sight to see, running for the house with a duck on my head. I have a vivid recollection of being terrified. I wrote about it in my book, *Variations on Herb*.

The boy is five, running for the farmhouse with a duck on his head. The duck is flapping his wings, beating the boy's ears, hauling at his scalp like a storm shingle hiking its nails. The boy is running, the duck on his head gyrating like a tin roof half torn off, the bill drinking blood. The boy is running, his mad hands flashing like a feather plucker in the belly down, the duck cleated so the toe webs are stretched open and rubbery, adhering to the flesh below the hair. The boy is running for the farmhouse where his grandfather is at the gate jacking the manure from his boots, first one, then the other, so the sheep dung is there on the jack blade whickered with straw, and dark green, Lincoln green, cud green, apple-shit green, a high sweet rose-garden stink instant and to be relished. The grandfather says nothing. With his eyes says, 'Don't hurt that duck, boy.' Says, 'Ducks are money.' With his eyes. Turns. Walks towards the house. Leaves the boy with a duck on his head like a living hat.

And though the truth of that day did not involve the presence of my grandfather, I know full well and truly that had he been there, he would have said, "Don't hurt that duck, boy." For though he loved me, he also knew the value of a living duck. I'd been where I shouldn't go. I'd been in duck country. As if for revenge, my uncle backed over the entire bevy and crippled them all in one fell swoop. They killed the injured and the maimed and plucked them all for future suppers. We've never had another living duck upon the farm until this day. The fly stickers grew heavy in a dozen rooms and my sister caught them in her hair with a gummy buzz. So much for ducks who kept the vermin down.

At the Fairs

MY PATERNAL GRANDFATHER, Herb, used to joke that there were only three seasons in Ontario—July, August, and winter—though of the three, I liked the summer least. The heat of early June brought on the crops and with the crops, the hay and with the hay, the seemingly endless tedium of toil in the fields. I mostly missed the labour of first cut, for I was still in school where we played inter-village ball and took our ease at spelling bees, math games and visual arts projects. But then the holidays arrived and I stayed home to work, which meant the coming on of wheat, the heavy loads of second cut, the harvesting of oats, the hoeing out of rain-weeds from the beans. Yet every year in late July we finally arrived at the lovely relief of early country fairs.

My father and uncle were slightly old-fashioned in their farming. They favoured the labour intensive threshing of grain and baling of hay. The hired man, Tom, and I followed the binder's first tough swath tossing sheaves clear of the second sweep of the field, while my uncle rode the binder setting the bed and watching the ties, while Dad drove the tractor with his expert concentration on the cut. After that first strike of acres, Tom and I were expected to go away and then return when the crop was cut and bound and ready to be stooked on end for curing. I can't imagine the despair of prairie sections, for it was bad enough for me to stand at the hot gate and regard our own sixteen-acre field littered with sheaves like war dead from a recent battle. It was cotton-gloved, long-sleeved, long-trousered, scratch-faced, hot, wet, dull, hard, stoop-backed work. At its worst, there were thistles gathered in the glean pricking through the straw to stab your hands, claw your breast, needle your inner arms, pierce your pocket places and scratch your reddened face. By wheat's end I was raw handed, flushed and defeated by the prospect of the oats yet to do.

All crop season, in the off hours, on days of rain we worked towards the fairs. We brought the best heifers in for fattening. We washed them week by week in creosote and water. We shone their halter buckles with Brasso and blackened cheesecloth rags and dragged the leather working it supple and dark with linseed oil. We painted the show-box. We painted the water pails and the grain pails and watched the rain. And then, in mid-August with the mows hay-heavy and barnyard stack fat and full of wheat gold and oat yellow and barn beam high with second cut where pigeons percolated and cooed and made their nests below the peaks, and we were ready for the first fairs of the season.

Showing sheep and cattle at livestock exhibitions had been a long-standing tradition on our farm and in our family. My grandfather, Herb, spoke in 1950 of the forty years he'd spent riding in boxcars and stock cars going to and from Chicago, Toronto and London. My family is the only family in history to have shown at the Royal Agricultural Winter Fair every year since it opened until the year the sheep were sold in 2000.

Every year, beginning with our first fair in Leamington, then Ridgetown, Dresden, the Toronto C.N.E., London, Brigden, Rockton, Alvingston, Glencoe, Petrolia, Shedden, Strathroy, Wallacetown, Simcoe, Ayr, and then the penultimate exhibition our own village school fair in Highgate, and finally for my family, but not for me, the Royal, capping the season in November in Toronto.

Although we no longer attended the Chicago International Livestock Exposition after I was born, it was one of the high points of the season for my grandfather. He was known as the 'Big Irishman from Canada.'

During the prohibition years he brought Canadian whiskey with him when he went and he was always generous with the spirits. One year he traded a bottle of Johnny Walker for several jackknives. He made the trade with a man known in the windy city as Jackknife

Benny. He'd traded for a few small boys' pocket knives and a few adult jackknives as gifts for friends, and he bought one special bone-handled beauty for himself.

One day my father was sent back the lane to cull the rye from the wheat. "Can I borrow your knife, Dad? Mine's too small for the work."

His Dad lent him the knife, with a caution to take care, for he wanted it returned in good condition. My father agreed. He went back the lane and like all boys good or bad grew quickly bored with the task at hand and began to play a game of toss and seek with his father's precious and expensive bone-handled knife. As would happen, he soon lost the knife in the wheat. Look as desperately as he might, he could not retrieve it. Rather than return to the barn sans knife, confess to a boyish carelessness and face his father's wrath, or worse, suffer his father's disappointment, my father pulled out his cotton pocket and cut the stitching to the lint with his own small boy's blade.

When he went up to the barn to report the completion of his assigned task, Grandpa immediately requested the return of his precious expensive bone-handled possession, the one he cherished, the one he'd bartered for from Jackknife Benny and brought home from Chicago. The one he'd thought to be the best in the shop, perhaps the best knife in the entire city—Plato's quintessential knife of knives. And grandfather would have known of such things since he was an avid reader of philosophy and might perhaps have been inclined to think even of knives in such Platonic terms.

My father reached into his pocket, looked surprised, pulled forth the slack and guilty cotton, fanned open the hole and noted the tear line marking the loss as an empty bargain with an accidental field. "It must have fallen out, Dad. See the hole. You can't blame me for that." Blame chance. Blame the gods of mending. Blame the pocket mites. Blame my mother's feckless thread, but don't blame me. Don't blame the boy who stands before you with his empty hands and ragged, pull-woven, guilty pockets.

Dad never told his own father the truth. His father went to his grave believing his son had simply lost a lovely knife to the mischief of poor clothing. It was a clever lie told by an equally clever liar. The lost knife makes my father laugh to tell it now.

Another memorable story from the days of showing sheep in Chicago involves the year, during the Depression, when one of my grandfather's gravid ewes lambed in the city. That was quite an unusual event in that she had been covered out of season. The lamb became the toast of Chicago. Every newspaper in the city sent a photographer to the exhibition grounds to snap her photograph. One clever photo-journalist called her, "Little Miss Chicago." She was front page news and her birth was a welcome diversion in hard times.

Grandpa did well at the exhibition in that difficult decade of poverty and deprivation. One year he sold a pen of ewes for enough money to buy additional land on the outskirts of the village. That second farm was ever-after known at home as 'the other place'. Whenever any-one in the family spoke of going to 'the other place,' we knew instantly that going there meant a half-mile journey from the farm to those fields bought with sheep money from the Depression years. That would remain the only occasion in the history of our flock involving the sale of the best breeding ewes.

I know Grandpa had only fond memories of his years as an exhibitor, and that he favoured those annual visits to Chicago above all others. In 1950, at a testimonial dinner held in his hon-our for his contribution to husbandry, he spoke only in the most glowing of terms of his hav-ing been premier showman, and most fondly of all of Chicago, home of proprietor Jackknife Benny, birthplace of 'Little Miss Chicago,' source of forty years of wonderful memories.

As for me, I preferred the cattle to the sheep, and in that my father was mostly the cattle-man and my uncle mostly the sheepman, that made sense. In my earliest memories of par-ticipating in the fairs, I remember myself as being the proud little boy, leading the ton-weight herd bull, Leeland Welcome, rocking down the truck ramp and into the fair barn while the townsfolk watched and praised my courage and my strength, saying, "Look at the little boy with that big bull. Isn't he brave?" Little did they know, I could have lain upon his ample back and pretended sleep, he was that gentle and good. I could have controlled his strength with the mere feckless tug of my smallest finger looped in his nose ring. I could have brought him lumbering down the chute like a tethered clutch of ten balloons, he was that tame and easy in his season.

Ridgetown

My father and uncle were both on the fairboard at Ridgetown, and so, every year, in the week before the fair was held, we drove to the grounds and participated in the preparation of the barns for the exhibition. My uncle was responsible for supervising the cleaning of the sheep pens and the making ready of the show ring. My father was involved in the sprucing up of the cattle barn. This work included raking smooth the earthen floor, opening the taps to freshen the water lines, setting up and tethering together fence sections for the sheep pens, sweeping the cement-floored alleys surrounding the indoor ring for the sheep show, white-washing the low beams and interior walls of the barns, and I was there to watch, to walk around, to breathe in the raised dust and lime fumes, to lean against a white gate, to linger and listen for the 'broom boy' commands of my elders. I was once called upon to open all the water taps and stay there with my empty bucket to wait out the knocks and clangs, the rush and hiss of air that spit and sputtered and exhaled in wet belches from the spigot, a final super-saturated eruption gushing forth banging at my pail bottom like a thirsty beast. "Don't drink the water from the tap, son," my father cautioned. "It's stale. The lines need to be let run to rid themselves of winter poisons."

And so, I stood holding my empty pail until with a sudden splash the pressure spewed and threw a stream that ushered from the faucet in a final torrent rushing in sudden gallons to the bucket bottom, rising to the rim to be carried and dumped out of doors. It was important work because when fair week arrived, it brought livestock in, and when the cattle came the stockmen expected a disinfected newness which they took for granted. Only a few of us knew the hours of hard work which had gone into the readying of things.

Our own cattle and sheep arrived by transport truck, and we followed in the pickup. We off-loaded the sheep at the sheep barn first, and then made our way to the north end of the horse barn leading our cattle thundering down the chute and through the horse alleys running the length of the racehorse stalls and from there through double doors to the cattle barn.

In those days, that is to say, in the late 1950s and early 1960s, the beef cattle were predominantly comprised of the three major old-country breeds—the Hereford, the Aberdeen Angus also know as the Black Angus, and the Shorthorns. Although the Hereford outnumbered other breeds at the city fairs, in many of the small town and village fairs, the Shorthorn cattle were the best represented of the three beef breeds. At Ridgetown, there were three or four exhibitors representing purebred Shorthorns. All herds were well-fitted for the show. We often found ourselves in competition with the same livestock at as many as a half-a-dozen fairs over the course of any given season. Each generation became friends with their contemporaries. And so, my sister and I were friends with the children of our father's competitors and our mothers were friends with fellow farmers' wives. We'd gather in the barns and joke and tease and cajole. We'd picnic out of our car trunks, sharing and trading like relatives. Rarely was a cross word spoken. We liked and respected one another and were fast friends.

This friendly atmosphere was broken only once that I can recall. At the south end of the beef barn, the dairy herds gathered. The men played the radio to stimulate the flow of milk and to calm the cattle in a strange environment. Their cow stalls smelled of fly spray and bag ban, and the Friesian bulls were cross. They stood eight foot at the shoulder with three chains running through double nose rings hooked to the stanchion wall. They affected a wild-eyed look of bovine madness. They bellowed and foamed and wagged their tongue froth so it came out in long thready sprays shaken at the world. They pawed deep holes in their earthen stalls so they sank to the girth on their forelegs and stood eye-level with passing children. Whenever anyone came near they took one backwards step, thus rising up and out of the hole as if they were growing out of the ground.

One year, at leaving time, we were walking our cattle through the horse alley on our way to the loading for home. A particularly arrogant and pushy Holstein breeder breezed past us almost knocking us down. His herd flowed past ours from bull to cow to heifer to calf to cow to calf to heifer as if they were a string of circus beasts hooked nose to tail and tail to nose. They were in fact a train of cattle beasts comprised of sixty four dew claws and thirty two legs. I could feel their hot silage breath and the milky sweep of their going . And when they were by us, they rushed up the loading ramp and essentially stole our ride.

The driver who was a friend of my father's seemed flabbergasted. He did not know quite what to say. He did not know what to make of what he'd seen. He'd been sent to pick up our cattle, but there he was with a Friesian load.

My father confronted the master of the interloping herd. "What do you think you're doing? That's my truck." The driver stood by in exasperated silence.

"I was there first," replied the owner of the Holsteins.

"You practically knocked my son down to get there," my father said.

"You can get another truck. I need to get home right away."

"You get you g.d. cattle off that truck right now! And you call the trucking company and order your own rig."

"There's another truck coming, George," the driver said by way of making the peace between these two strangers.

"Is this the truck sent to pick up my cattle or not?" My father asked.

"It's your truck, George," the driver said. "But what am I going to do? This gentleman here has his cattle loaded already."

My father turned his wrath on the dairy man and said, "You heard him. Get your cattle off my truck." By this time the two men were shouting and enraged.

"I was in a concentration camp in the war," said the dairy man, as if that were relevant, as if that excused every discourtesy, as if his suffering earned him first place in every line he ever attended to, as if having been a victim of fascist repression would excite a sympathetic hearing from my father who was by now in no mood to bargain.

"You should have died there!" my father shouted.

In the end, we waited for the second truck which arrived an hour later. In the end, the transport owner let us know that the Holstein man did not pay his bills, nor would he ever again be allowed to transport his cattle on the owner's rigs. And that was the first, last and only occasion of his exhibiting his herd at Ridgetown fair. It is the only occasion I can recall the hearing of cross words in the cattle barn.

I had heard many disagreements in the past, but never with such bitterness and acrimony. When I think back, I find myself wondering why that dairy man felt he had the right to push his way past us. And now, with what I know of concentration camps of the last great war, I wonder why he felt the need to mention his having been in one. And my father's words still sting. "You should have died there," burn into the past like fire in dry paper.

A few years later, the son of the transport company owner took up truck driving for his father. He brought our cattle home from a fair and drove into the village for supper after he dropped our cattle off. He had worked up quite a thirst over the closing hours of the day. He pulled a soft drink from the cooler, popped the cap and drank a healthy draft of cold soda pop. He didn't notice, until he felt the burning in his throat, that the bottle had been tampered with. The pop had been replaced by pure acid. He suffered very severe throat burns and nearly died. It was discovered that a disgruntled factory worker had tampered with the soda pop. It was years before the young truck driver recovered from the damage to his esophagus.

Two other incidents come to mind from that particular fair. I remember my dad backing up his half-ton and asking me to keep watch on my side to be sure he didn't run the side panel into the door jamb. I couldn't see very well with only the window down, so I opened the door on my side, leaning out a little, holding on by the arm rest, watching the jamb glide past the truck box, keeping my father assured that he would not scrape the paint until I heard a soft metallic crunch and saw the buckle and warp of the door panel as the open door came into contact with the barn door jamb. In that instant I realized that I was smart boy stupid.

My father screamed and the panel wowed and wobbled and sprung its hinges against my good intentions. Until the day we sold that truck, it blamed me every time it wobbled open and crunched closed with the wind in the frame like a whistle.

On another occasion, a good friend of mine and I were killing an hour on the midway on a slow afternoon just before shutdown. Our favourite ride was otherwise empty and there was no one waiting in line. We paid our fare and mounted the steps and sat together in what appeared to be the best of the best cars on the Tilt-a-Whirl. Usually only a minute-long scramble, our ride lasted fifteen minutes. The cruel carnie left us swirling and whirling and turning and spinning and circling in variations of fast gyres and slow swivels until my friend became so sick-dizzy he tested the centrifugal laws of physics by puking in a green and vomitous projection hurling the entire content of his gut on the wind. When we finally came to a stop, neither of us could stand. We were both nauseous and disoriented as rats in raw silage. We were cheap-wine sick. Sea sick. We had entirely lost our appetite for gravity. My mother took us home where we convalesced on my double bed as on a dizzy swell of ocean crest and trough, crest and trough in easy weather trying to read comic books in that tidal motion. Eventually the floor went solid and the walls went still. If you've ever tried to stand athwart the gunnels of a tippy canoe or rocking row boat in a shallow wave, you'll know what walking was for us that day. If you've ever drunk a demijohn of inexpensive wine, or mixed a single swig of whiskey with a first cigar, you'll know the affect of fifteen minutes on the Tilt-a-Whirl at Ridgetown fair, with Johnny Rivers on the wind to catch your breakfast as it swims and thinning circle going green like the particle rings of the planet singing, "this is your skull as a gyroscope, this is your brain as a spinning spool."

The loading

Though the sheep were sometimes transported to the fairs in the half-ton pickup with the rack on the back, more often than not the sheep and cattle were taken to the show on a transport truck. The cattle were loaded first, tethered to the wall in the front of the trailer and separated by a metal gate which swung out from the left wall and closed on the right. Then we'd load either the rams or the ewes segregating them by gender with a partition. Finally we'd load the hay, the grain sacks, the water pails, feed pails, straw bales and halter box for the show.

On rare occasions, I'd be allowed to ride in the cab with the driver, my father and my uncle. However, that was often problematic what with the three full grown men and a growing boy crowding the cab. It was especially uncomfortable and awkward because I'd be in the way of the gear shift. It wasn't too bad for a short ride, but for a long haul it was particularly unpleasant and an irritation to the driver shifting gears and knocking my knees as he ground a tough meshing of cogs up a difficult hill.

More often, I'd get up and ride in the back with the beasts. Sometimes I'd sit on a bale, sometimes on a turned-over pail. On one occasion, my cousin Ted and I rode the three hours all the way from Highgate to Toronto in the trailer while my father, uncle and the driver occupied the cab.

Ted, who was more inclined towards mischief than I, noticed that there were trap doors in the roof of the trailer. He and I climbed the gate and flipped open one of the vents in the ceiling. Ted poked his head and shoulders up and took the wind full on his body like a dog with his head out the window of a rushing car. He encouraged me to do the same, and though I was more timid than he, I took the bait and went shouldering up just as we rushed beneath an overpass which seemed only inches from my windswept hair. It seemed it might have topped me like a soft boiled breakfast egg, were I but only a forehead taller. In a single petrified motion, I jumped from sky to floor, leaving Ted laughing at me for a coward. In my mother's words, "we were always up to no good." Whenever we were together Ted and I would do things I'd never dare alone. In all the dozens of times I'd ridden in those trailers, it had never occurred to me to test the roof vents. Ted was fearless and being fearless Ted was fun. He'd wanted to see what I'd seen. He still wanted to climb the gate and look out on decapitation. I refused to allow it.

He and I had been known to spit on strangers from above in the spectator stands at the horse races. We'd blown air into the tito mast of a standing two-seater aeroplane at an air show to see the air speed needle jump in the cockpit until we were caught by the owner. He threatened to tell our parents and we hid all day rather than be punished by our fathers for our mischief.

Riding in the back of a transport truck full of show-ring cattle beasts and prize-winning Lincoln longwool sheep was always a loud, rattly, cattle-lowing, sheep-bleating, road-humming, gear-grinding, body-shaking affair. It made all conversation nearly impossible, not only because it was difficult to hear a human voice above the animal din, but also because the voice quavered with road rut and the hard ride, so words came out shaken as if by grief or bad nerves.

One of the most peculiar rides I was ever on occurred when a local character and poetry reciter, Blake F., asked to be given a ride to Wallacetown Fair. He took along his black old fashioned, high-handled man's bike because he planned to cycle the thirty miles home rather than inconvenience us. Famous in the local gathering places for his mumbled recitations of doggerel learned in elementary school, he'd just given a performance for CFCO radio in Chatham, and he'd also performed for an English class in Ridgetown. A septuagenarian bachelor who shaved only on Sundays, he lived in an unpainted clapboard house in the village. Whenever he spoke, however close I was to him, I never caught much more than one word in ten. His voice was almost a whisper. He'd speak in a low drone of slurred consonants and dragged vowels as if he were a tractor idling.

Though his speech was not quite as odd to me as another family's, where one family member said, "I see, I see, uh huh, uh huh, I see," whose wife said, "however, however, however," and whose cousin muttered, " 'nd that, 'nd that, 'nd that," with every exhale. In my imagination, I'd heard this family once at table speaking to one another in partial sentences without ever uttering a single coherent thought. "I see, I see, uh huh, uh huh," "however, however," " 'nd that, 'nd that, 'nd that," "I see, uh huh, uh huh," and so on ad infinitum. Nevertheless, Blake had a reputation as something of a poet, though he wrote no poems and his recitals were entirely unintelligible. After he'd visited the secondary school English class and given a recital, with the typical murmur of his delivery slurring the words into a flat elision of language as if he were stone drunk, a marble-mouthed rendering of Robert Service muttered like melting, the phrases flowing from his mouth like pooling wax tallowing down on Sam McGee's frozen corpse, one of the students was overheard to say with awe, "he must be a poet, I didn't understand a single word."

And so, Blake was on board the cattle truck with his bicycle, all the show stock and me. And he didn't stop talking the entire half-hour the whole way there. He looked right at me, and I didn't catch a single word. I could hear by the rhythms of his speech, that he was practising the metres of bad verse he meant to share with the fairgoers at Wallacetown, which I knew from my father's brag, had some mixture of pride and resentment for having been close to the place where world-famous economist John Kenneth Galbraith had been born and come of age.

I listened politely as I would to the bleating of a troubled ram. I knew Blake planned on taking the show-ring stage after the cattle exhibition was over. He was planning a recital over the fairboard P.A. I don't think the fair board knew what they were in for when they'd agreed to allow Blake to recite. Already radio famous, he was excited by the opportunity to show his stuff.

Unfortunately for Blake, there had been some sort of miscommunication. Sadly, no one had bothered to tell the guardians of the P.A. system to provide a time slot for Blake's memory work. And someone decided, after having been given a private audience with Blake, not to allow him access to the microphone. Although I understood and sympathized with their obviously legitimate reservations, I was disappointed on Blake's behalf. His excitement turned to sorrow. His shoulders sagged and he rode out the fairground gate and into the distance pumping homeward in the muttering whistle of himself and the wind that stirred the roadside chicory, the ditch weed Queen Anne's Lace, and made a ghostly rattle of mock applause in the yellow-leafed spectre of early fall corn.

◆

Each Labour Day weekend, I missed one day of school to help my father on Tuesday, which was show day at London Fair. That same day was also a holiday for city school-age children so they might attend the fair. The year of my sixteenth birthday, my cousin brought along a few of her classmates and they visited the cattle barn. Two sisters lingered a while and I knew from the way they were behaving that they found me 'kind of cute.' One of them sat down on the bale next to me and sidled up so close I could feel her body heat. I was a shy lad who didn't say much when girls were around. But I fell for her, partly because I was flattered, partly because she was very pretty with long brown hair and a ready smile, and mostly because I was almost sixteen. A few months later, those same sisters accompanied my relatives on a Sunday visit to the farm in the late spring. I entertained them with my best Curly Howard imitation and they giggled encouragement, my favourite girl saying, "Say 'soit-en-ee' again, Johnny," and so I repeated, "Soit-en-ee, soit-en-ee," like a parlour parrot as we all laughed under the laundry line. The summer of love came and went and I pined until Labour Day arrived and with it the fair. I'd worked my way through another year of warm days and cool September mornings that typified the weather of early September at London Fair. At five a.m., the dew was chill on the fences, the air cool and damp, but I could wait. Tuesday would arrive and I would see her again. Sure enough, Tuesday came, and with it my cousin and her girlfriends paid a visit to the cattle barn. The girl whom I'd been thinking about all summer was there as well. I'd become the twitter-pated lad, waiting for Labour Day to arrive with its annual visit from the girl who thought I was cute. Perhaps there was evidence to the contrary, but in the narcissus of her eyes, I was handsome enough to be worthy of young love.

When she arrived, she approached me smiling and chatty as ever, but I had grown so horribly self-conscious by then, I'd lost all the hubris of boyhood. I simply stood there stunned and stone tongued staring at my own two feet. The last words I recall her ever uttering in my presence were, "What's wrong with him?" Meaning, why won't he even say hello. And so they went on their way and forgot me. I never saw her again.

◆

I was always a good and a dutiful boy. My actions were informed by a profoundly moral sense of absolute right and wrong. Though too shy to speak my mind to a girl, I would rise to an occasion and show an uncommon generosity or courage. As a little boy, I read the Bible after church most Sundays. I was a server in the local Anglican church. I even dreamed of one day becoming a man of the cloth. I used to read my grandfather's books. One particular book, a translation of the writings of Spinoza, appealed to my sense of right and wrong. I read a passage of Spinoza's thoughts on redemption and once engaged in a fifteen-minute debate at Leamington Fair at a Bible booth with a man who thought me precocious. Years later, my nephew gave me a copy of a book by Spinoza, the lens grinder, and I found out that Spinoza and I were both born on November 24th. I remember as a six-year-old boy thinking, when I grow up, I'm going to open a grocery store and give everything away to the customers. Then the poor children in our village school won't have to steal candy. Perhaps I was feeling guilty over my 'current events' contribution when I stood up in class and delivered the news, "Brenda O. steals," and then sat down. I had heard that news at the supper table the night before and I found it quite interesting and worthy of the attention of the teacher and the class. The moment those cruel words were out of my mouth, I knew they were somehow inappropriate. My mother told me that one year, when I was given money for the midway at Highgate Fair, that I spent it all on gifts for the family. I bought something for my mother, and something for my visiting aunt.

I'm quite fond of that little lad with the old soul. I lay no claim to his goodness. The greatest test of my courage came in the nineteen sixties when young men began to let their hair grow long. Eventually I would grow an Afro that would fill a doorway, but while I was still at home, I was required to keep my hair above my ears and if it dared to touch my collar, I was immediately sent to the barber's. However, one year I refused and my father let it go. I remember hurtful comments from men I'd known all my life. One fellow said, "George, how can you put your feet under the same table as that thing?" pointing at me. Another acquaintance called me a "hootchie kootchie girl' and suggested I might consider wearing a grass skirt. One of my great-uncles said of me the summer I let my hair grow past my collar, "he has respect for neither God nor country," and thus condemned me to my own private den of iniquity.

That same year, I joined my father as always at London Fair. There was a young man in his late teens working a broom in the cattle barns. He was part of a group of temporary workers hired by the fairboard to sweep the alleys and keep the manure clear so the visitors wouldn't foul their shoes walking through. He had long hair growing half-way down his spine.

A few of the exhibitors were drinking beer in the alleyway between the cattle stanchions. They worked up a drinker's courage, grabbed him by his locks, dragged him hair first into the alley, threw him down like an upended sheep and with a chattering of electric sheers cut a swath of baldness from the nape of his neck to the centre of his skull so he was partly tonsured like a half-scalped hippie on his way to Vietnam. When they let him go, he simply sat up under their laughter, took out a mouth organ and blew mournful music, with slow tears rolling down his cheeks.

I ran outside and found a policeman on foot patrol near the barns. There was an officer on duty every day near the exit doors. I reported the scoundrels who'd participated in this awful deed. I knew the names of every man involved. Had known them all my life till then. The officer came inside, made his observations, interviewed the victim who seemed mostly mute and unwilling to tell much about what had happened. None were ever charged with a crime. The young man was summarily fired because, in the words of the livestock men, "long hair scares the cattle." As for me, I was regarded by all as someone who had betrayed the men. The next morning, one of the perpetrators, a forty-year-old Hereford breeder, accosted me in the washroom. He came over to where I was grooming, looked me in the eye in the mirror like a conversation in a barber's chair, and said, by way of threat and reward for my betrayal, "You're next!" With those three words he walked out, leaving me alone with my fears.

I spent the next two days looking over my shoulder for the clip that never came. I cannot help compare these cowards to the lynch mobs of the world. And I do not regret reporting them. Though they were my fellow showmen, I did not like them for what they had done. I look back and refuse alliance. In some way, I wish they had made good the threat to clip my hair. It would have been a bald badge of honour.

If I think about their victim, I recall how he drew forth his mouth organ and breathed a mournful music as he softly wept. I wonder where he is and what became of him and what he thinks of the cattle men who caught him and cut his hair against his wishes.

The Cattle Show

When I was very young I believed that Paris, Ontario, and Paris, France, were one and the same place. I had my own private summer in our Paris when my father was called upon to judge the cattle show at Paris Fair. I remember riding there with my father at the wheel telling my sister and me, "Stop all that reading. Open your eyes and look around you. You've never seen this part of the country before. Stop wasting your time with your noses in books. Look out the window and see the world."

When we finally arrived in Paris and came down the hill into town overlooking the river, I remember wondering what all the fuss had been about concerning the so-called 'city of lights'. This didn't look very different from most other small towns within my experience. Indeed, I preferred the well-treed beauty of Ridgetown. It would be years before I realized there were two Paris's, the one occupied by Parisians, the other by Parisites, or so the local joke would have it.

On another occasion of my father's foray into judging, we stopped at a restaurant on our way home from Simcoe, where the Norfolk County Fair had been held. My mother was unimpressed with the restaurant's atmosphere and decor, but father ruled, so in we went. After we ordered our meals, Dad and I descended the narrow stairs to use the basement facilities. I suppose we might have suspected that this was not a classy joint when they'd told us they had no hot dog buns and said they'd serve the dogs cut lengthwise on hamburg buns. When we arrived at the bottom step and our shoes touched cold cement at the base of the stairs, we heard a squawking from the corner in shadow just beyond the light. That squawking was coming from a live chicken on the run from a cook wielding a sharpened butcher's wedge. The bloody-aproned cook came chopping out of the darkness just behind a white flurry of fear and feathers flapping her wings as if she might indeed learn to fly. That doomed hen left a strong impression on my young mind. It would be years later before I realized that the town we were in was Delhi. My first teaching job was in Waterford, in Norfolk County only a few kilometres from Delhi. The year we were on strike, my good friend George

O'Leary and I edited the strike newsletter. We spent our Thursdays driving the county to the five high school communities delivering the newsletter to the staff strike centres. George enjoyed stopping for lunch at a small restaurant in Delhi. That restaurant where we ate every Thursday turned out to be the same restaurant where I'd seen that poor hen lose her life in the basement by the men's room. My small world suddenly shrank like hen moult plucked in steam heat, the image of my red-handed mother fowled to the wrist with memory.

Dresden

It's hard to believe it of my Ontario, but there used to be a law on the books in the town of Ridgetown prohibiting a black man from staying overnight within town limits. To my knowledge, the law was never enforced, but it did echo back to the days of the Underground Railway when southwestern Ontario was a major destination for runaway slaves. There was a proposal for very strict laws called Larwill's Laws, drafted in the 1840's for fear of the arriving blacks. The Chatham man behind those laws was a man named Edwin Larwill, who said of his own children that he would rather see them dead than have them go to school with black children. Emancipationist, John Brown, planned his Harper's Ferry Raid in the city of Chatham before returning to the States to be captured and hung for the crime of high treason. So, the area from which I come, though rich in history, is not exclusively rich in the proud traditions of tolerance and equality which are often associated with Canada.

Much like Ridgetown, Dresden's small annual livestock fair ran for three days from Thursday through Saturday in late July and early August. Because Dresden was a little over forty-five minutes by car from home, we always stayed overnight at the fairgrounds. My father and I slept in the bed of the pickup truck. We shook out two bales of clean, new straw for ticking. We covered that prickled surface with a well-worn quilt and slept in blue, three-season sleeping bags. We parked the truck in a grass lot reserved for overnight exhibitors. Each evening long after dark, we made a final check of the cattle, crossed the grassy parking lot and retired between eleven and midnight. We fell asleep to the sounds of the midway, which besides the rattle-round of Conklin show's machines—the Tilt-a-Whirl, the Ferris

Wheel, the Round Up—I heard the thrill-screams of the young shrieking round and round with wild delight, and I heard the music of the day, Tom Jones, Chuck Berry, Petula Clark, Motown, the Beatles, Johnny Rivers and more.

I lay beside my father, falling into dream on the crush and gentle thistle prick and straw scratch of summer. One particular night on the way to take our rest, walking the dark jigsaw of exhibitors' vehicles, we heard a commotion coming from a parked car. We approached the car occupied by three sheep men and one cattle man. Two old shepherds sat in the back, casual as you please, smoking their pipes and imbibing from cheap drinking flasks. You could smell the Borkum Riff and Cutty Sark aroma of sweetly burning burley and distilled alcohol as the two men sat quietly and contemplatively puffing their meershaums and sipping their booze like bucolic philosophers considering a secret in separate, deeply satisfied silence. They appeared to be gently and slightly amused and were entirely mum, as if unaware or unconcerned or certainly detached and completely uninvolved with the drama going on before them glimpsed through the smoke haze. And the imbroglio on the front seat had definitely drawn our attention, if not theirs.

Either these two elderly sheep men in the rear seat were stupefied by liquor, or they simply thought what was going on before their eyes was none of their concern. They were watching it as boys watch All Star Wrestling on TV. What drew our attention was the fact that the two men in the front seat were fighting tooth and nail. My father immediately apprised himself of the affair and said, "What the hell's going on here!?" He knew all four participants. The two disengaged pipe smokers nodded recognition, mouthing "Hello George" round their pipe stems, exhaling his whispered name. The men in the front seat were obviously locked in drunken combat and the altercation, though not staged for our amusement, seemed to escalate with our arrival.

The two inebriates were grappling like greased up wrestlers, the one having the other in a head lock. The smaller man was on top, choking the larger who, by the time we arrived, was turning red and gasping and wheezing and making strangle sounds. He was obviously entering the last stages of consciousness before the final suffocation. My father leaned in through the open window, locked his arm around the skinny shoulders of the upper man and pulled him off. The object of this runt's strangulation sat up, took a greedy insuck of desperate air, as my father held the lean fellow until the little man loosened and released his rage.

For the next few moments the two grapplers sat in silence. The one rubbing his throat, breathing deeply, and looking around for the mickey he'd dropped while fighting. The smaller of the two sat seething in a wordless mixture of rage and shame. "Now get out of the car and get the hell out of here," my father said, opening the door. The man emerged like a beaten dog. He raced off tail-tucked and chastened with water-feathers of foam and drool dripping down his chin.

Since that evening, every time my father sees the man he'd rescued, that man says, "Thanks, George. Do you remember the time you saved my life? That little prick would have killed me if you hadn't pulled him off. I was going under."

As it is, no one liked the small lean rib count of a man who'd had my father's friend in the sleeper of a choke hold. Even the other sheep men treated him gentle but strange. And no one was surprised to hear they'd locked him up for being drunk and disorderly. That same year he was arrested for exposing himself to city women in the fair barns at the CNE.

In the mornings at Dresden Fair, we woke and stripped to the waist and washed our upper bodies in cold water splashed from pails we'd filled from the cattle taps and carried sloshing to our truck. My father shaved in the chill, rinsed his razor in soap blue liquid and watched his face reflected in the side mirror of the truck. I asked my father recently if he ever remembered going a single day without shaving. He said he didn't. Even in hospital, he insists on a clean shave and waits for the nurses to groom him.

We did our morning chores first, then washed up, then joined the other stock men at a restaurant in downtown Dresden. Because we were working men, we ate in the atmospheric kitchen rather than at the regular tables out front. The two short-order cooks were talkative and amusing. To quote my Dad, "they never stopped talking." The older of the two was perhaps sixty years of age. He was short and slightly plump. The younger was about six feet tall with black hair. Like many dark-haired men, he had a clean-shaven beard shadow, and he was very amusing and engaging. They both wore long white cook's aprons that went chin to shin and were tied in the back with a cotton sash. Unlike contemporary kitchen hygiene, neither man wore a cook's cap and their aprons were splashed with grease and dappled with egg yolk. The restaurant smelled of busy breakfast. It was aromatic with the hot sizzle of side bacon and country fresh eggs cracked one-handed and let leak into a perfect yolk-yellow pool that bubbled an instant orange-white on the sere of a flat griddle. The empty shells flew through the air and landed with an exact and unwavering precision of performance right in the open-topped trash can close by. These men were accustomed to being watched at work. They cooked breakfast and ceaselessly jabbered and yammered like a staged play.

From the first time I went there, I became their favourite audience. They liked performing for an appreciative and impressed young lad like me. They looked my way when they spoke their lines. They juggled eggs for my amusement. They called them 'cackle berries' and popped them, muscled arm to waiting palm. They spun coins on my placemat, called me 'young fella' saying, "What does the young fella want this morning?" They did what my mother refers to as 'making a fuss,' and I loved being the object of their attention. I think I loved them. For a long while afterwards, they remained one of my favourite memories of the fairs. Each year, I looked forward to making their reacquaintance. They entertained the breakfast hour and made the butter better on their flashing knives.

Years later, after I'd left home for good, when my oldest cousin came of marrying age, we found ourselves in need of a meal because Al's reception did not include the cousins, though the wedding did. I importuned my relatives to go to Dresden for supper. I wanted to introduce them to my experience of the restaurant I remembered from my boyhood. I thought perhaps I might recapture some of the drama of those fair-morning breakfasts, even if only to say hello to the two cooks I'd come to enjoy. The first disappointment upon arrival arose from the fact that the kitchen was out-of-bounds at the supper hour. I had hoped we might be able to meet the cooks. That was not to be. We were shown to an unextraordinary booth typical of most family restaurants in the province. It was all shiny grey arborite and polished, turquoise Naugahyde. The bread-loaf sized juke box sang Hank Snow for a quarter. The ketchup bottle stood as red sentinel next the salt and pepper shakers and the dessert menu with its unnatural-looking photograph of apple pie. The menus offered normal fare. Hot beef sandwiches floating in oleaginous gravy. Chicken with a single ice-cream scoop of mashed potatoes topped by toffee-brown liquid grease. Each page contained a laminate snapshot of one item. The waitress did not smile, but rather stood by in silence, snapping her pen and giving us each an impatient glance. She went away and returned delivering ice shivers of tap water in slightly cloudy drinking glasses.

She left us there to consider our options. To say the least, I was gravely disappointed and slightly embarrassed to have insisted that we go there. As it turned out, there was absolutely nothing in the experience to recommend the place. When we'd entered, I'd noticed a young black family seated in a booth. I knew that Dresden had been a major destination for black families fleeing slave states, but I was blissfully unaware of the local bigotry. I knew about the proximity of the museum which had been the home of escaped slave, Josiah Henson. I knew that the region was the home of many rightly proud black families with an heroic heritage. I did not know about the local racism.

So there we sat, my sister, my cousins and I, regarding our menus, when I began to watch the young black family who had arrived and been seated in a nearby booth before we had arrived. I saw that they were being conspicuously ignored by the waitress. We had our water. They had none. We had our menus. They went without. We received our colas. They were being passed by in the to and fro of the not-too-busy waitress. Finally, as if the oversight were not deliberate, the young father politely called her over. She paused, performed a perfunctory half-step in their direction, stood over their table, and matter-of-factly said, "We don't serve your kind here." And it was 1969. It was the day I first heard the Rolling Stones recording of "Honky Tonk Women". And this was my Ontario. This wasn't Selma, Alabama where the brutal police washed good people from the streets with fire hoses. This wasn't Memphis and the death of heroes good and true, shot from their shoes on motel balconies by repugnant bigots. This wasn't Johannesburg's apartheid. This was my county, my province, my country, my home, my town, and these were my people. I was so ashamed. We didn't finish our meal, but we did pay our bill. I had been so fond of the two short-order cooks. It broke my heart to think how hateful a place this was. I'd read Harper Lee's novel and thought of that fictional town and those racist feelings as far-away and morally inferior. Now I knew we were no better than our neighbours to the far south. Even today, when I hear the cow bell intro to the lovely Rolling Stones' song, the one I heard first on that very day, I'm taken back to the memory of how those small-town Ontario values I'd been raised with were poisoned by the same ugly prejudices most often associated with elsewhere.

Another painful memory of Dresden goes to the summer when one of the Shorthorn families brought an older American cousin to the fair. Phillip was nineteen and it was the era of the draft. His call-up came that summer and he was paying one last visit to his cousins before going off to boot camp. He seemed handsome to the girls and super-sophisticated to the rest of us who were not so much younger than he. He smoked a pipe and had an easy smile. We all sat talking the afternoon away, kicking our heels on the halter box and hay bales and falling in love with summer life. My cousin Bill met his future bride there that same summer. I bought a package of cigarettes and smoked them at home, typing away in my bedroom. My mother came up the stairs and caught me in a cloud of fumes. She never told Dad. My sister was dating a boy from town who rode a motor scooter. I'd suffer my first adolescent crush that same year in September. What hung over us all that summer was the fact that when the fair was over, Phillip was bound for the war.

We laughed a lot together. There were about eight of us who were fast friends. We worked and joked and shared each other's company with joy. And what we Canadians knew of the war was only that the Americans seemed to believe in something which made no sense to any of us. I remember we'd asked our high school history teacher to tell us why the Americans were fighting in Vietnam. He gave us a thoughtful and well-informed answer, the central argument of which involved the domino theory. I think we were correct to be perplexed and unpersuaded. We knew there was either something hidden from our view, or something with which we did not agree. We mostly thought that the Americans were just wrong about the world. But Phillip had lost the conscription lottery. And he believed in the dictum, "my country right or wrong." He looked forward to a youthful adventure. He saw going to war as simply 'doing his duty.' I looked him in the eye and thought to myself, "You might not survive another year."

Two summers hence, I heard he had returned alive, but changed. His cousins did not speak of him at all. His aunts spoke in quiet and tragic tones. He'd returned a drug addict and a drunk. He'd become a family outcast. He'd seen too much. He'd seen a friend decapitated next to him. He'd seen men pierced cap-a-pied with sharpened punji sticks. Little wonder we did not ever see him again.

I could not reconcile this loss, this suffering, this soldier's heart affliction, this man of the mile-long gaze, with the boy I'd come to know that easy summer at Dresden Fair. Through him I saw my own good fortune to have been born to a different nation.

Had it not been for the fairs, there at the cow tails and sheep docks of my youth, I'd never have had my own taste of war. I'd seen Vietnam in the shake-out of straw. I'd fallen in love in the redolence of hay. I'd seen racism in the water-pail reflection of my own sad face. I'd felt the wrath of red necks in the chatter of sheep shears. I'd heard the murmur of doggerel in the rattle of truck tin. I'd been given the gift of going away with the knowledge of being fully in the world. The connection between sweet molasses and rolled oats and the Mekong Delta and the Mason-Dixon Line was formed and fused by the grand adventure of growing up close to the show ring. I was of that world, and I'd carry that world with me out and into the world beyond my own small acres.

Freak Show

When we went to the CNE, we slept on beds in the men's quarters located just off the hog pens in the fair barns. I shared a room with my father and a few other exhibitors. We usually rose at four a.m. so that we might have time to complete our morning chores before the fair crews arrived to clean the alleys and buck out the barns.

We walked our ten lowing cattle outside and tied them up to a fence that ran the length of the barn along the north wall of the building. We forked away the night's accretions of cow flap and wet straw, shook out fresh bedding, cleaned and currycombed and exercised the cattle beasts and then walked them back indoors, tied them with a halter-chain jangle to the wall ring, watered them, fed them each a fistful of rolled oats and molasses, shook out a single flake of the best second-cut hay per beast, surveyed our work, leaned on the fork awaiting a few morning constitutionals, and gathered briefly in circles of conversation with the other men, our hands smelling of grain meal and burnt-sugar molasses, saddle soap and creosote, and the sweet dry-grasses and gold straw dusts of summer.

Our early-morning chores required between two and three hours of satisfactory labour before we earned our own breakfast. The work was never finished until the cattle were fed. A few final details were often required. A gathering up of the last grain pail from the greedy rough tongue of some heifer licking the galvanized inner silver for the possibility of one last lingering oat clinging to the metal seam on the mottled swirl of an outer weld, her halter chain ringing against the rim as she worked her hungry jaw. Or just as we were about to leave, the herd bull lifts his tail and drops a feed-rich, aromatically splendid dung flop to be turned under and left for later. Meanwhile an arch-backed female floods her bedding with a hot yellow stream of piss that might stain her white flanks if it's not dragged clear and carried off as a fork full of super-soak to the wheelbarrow at the end of the row.

We usually went for ham and eggs at the nearby Junior Farmers' food tent, but I remember one occasion when we joined the sheep men, crowded into a truck cab and bed and about ten of us went off the grounds for a morning feast at a nearby restaurant. We gathered up tables enough to accommodate all, and sat around, talking, joking, and poking fun at the world. We were country men in the city, superior to everything in every direction. Better for the nature of our work. Better for our knowledge of the field. Better for our prize stock. Better for our life in the quiet, remoter regions of rural Ontario. Better for the lanolin scent of our hands and on our clothing. Better for everything about us. The city was privileged by our presence. And this table promised a breakfast bounty, the bacon from our hogs, the eggs from our hens, the toast from our grains, the coffee from our mountain brothers in the hill plantations of Costa Rica, Colombia, and Brazil.

As my father once said to an urban uncle with whom he had been conversing all day, "Art, we've been talking for hours. We've been discussing everything under the sun, and I've come to a conclusion."

"What's that George?"

"The best thing you can eat is food," Dad said laughing. He loves to tell that story. When he relates it, he says how Uncle Art laughed to hear the punch line. The moral makes the farmer the unsung hero of the world. Without food, we would perish. Without farmers, we would have no food. The hand that tills the earth, feeds the city.

So there we were, sharing the glory of being ourselves in the city when the waitress arrived to take our order. It was immediately obvious to me that she knew most of this crew where everyone seemed to be talking at once. She travelled round the table with her eyes and took each order with a nod and without writing anything down. She joked along with laughing eyes, memorized our breakfasts with a casual ease and walked away smiling.

Ten or fifteen minutes later she delivered our meals, each exact request arriving in front of the correct recipient without pause, hesitation or the possibility of error. This feat was as amazing as any magic show I've ever seen. To this day, I haven't the slightest notion as to how she achieved such perfection surrounded as she was by our deliberate chaos. She'd delivered what we'd asked for without seeming to listen, while we kibitzed, and teased, and cajoled, and joked, and changed our minds about peameal and butter, pancakes and toast, and choice of juice. When she walked away, leaving us to our clatter, my uncle leaned over and asked me, "Do you know who that is?"

"No," I said, perhaps expecting to learn that she was internationally famous in the world of waitressing.

"That is Johnny Bower's sister."

I must confess I was impressed by that fact. Johnny Bower was the goal tender for the Stanley Cup winning Toronto Maple Leafs hockey team. However, I was more impressed by something these men seemed to have failed to notice. If Johnny Bower might have thrilled any red-blooded Canadian boy with a word or a pat on the head or an autographed hockey card, surely his sister was equally impressive in the less-celebrated world of waitressing. Or so I thought. I was a boy she'd barely noticed, sitting among men, eating bacon and eggs and wishing I might tell her, "I think Johnny Bower's your brother, not the other way round." He might be pleased to be thought of that way. When the pucks are bouncing off his forehead, he might feel blessed to think of his sister and the glory of eggs-over-easy set beside a sunny-side-up served firm not runny order, plate for plate perfect, cup for cup and glass for glass like a shut out, a season-winning save in the simplicity of squeezed oranges and only slightly sour grapefruit flavour of an ideal morning.

One year, my cousin Ted came with us to be company for me and to help with the work. We stayed out late, walking the midway without any money to spend. We didn't go on any of the rides. We didn't play Guess-the-Month and win a Kewpie doll. We didn't squirt the clown's mouth with water to bust the balloon for a stuffed toy. We simply walked the circuit looking at the girls. We were just that age when girls didn't notice us, but we noticed them. We were dumb farm boys out gawking at city girls.

We came up with a stupid idea for jostling through the midway crowd. We walked 'elbows out' with the thought of brushing up against breasts in what seemed to us an innocent and inadvertent grazing of mammary flesh. Perhaps this might seem a violation in retrospect, but to a thirteen-year-old boy, it was an opportunity too good to miss. "Excuse me. Excuse me," we would say if the need arose, though it never did. Was that a bosom I felt along the hairs in the crook of my bent arm? I hope so, I'd think, though I haven't a clue.

Ted and I stayed out late. We walked the midway until shut down which was one a.m., then we went quietly to bed. This late-night gallivanting was a bad idea because Dad was always awake and cheerful and ready for the day at four in the morning. There's nothing quite like being awoken after a mere three hours sleep by a man who is well-rested and enthusiastic about the prospects of the day when it's still dark outdoors. But I was a dutiful son. I got up and went to chores however grudgingly and sluggish with fatigue. Ted, on the other hand, didn't rise. He rolled over, grumbled and stayed put.

"You can't get that damned boy out of bed," my father would say to me as if I were to blame. "What's wrong with him?"

It wasn't the work I took exception to. It was the good cheer. Like the mother in Tennessee Williams' *Glass Menagerie*, there was too much, "rise and shine, rise and shine" about him. That night, Ted and I conspired. We poured two cans of Coke, one in each boot, after my father had gone to bed. Then we went out for another midway romp. When we retired, we giggled ourselves to sleep with the prospect of morning.

In the early hours, my father rose, saying, "Time to get up, boys. The day is wasting." And then I heard the sock slosh and his anger in the dark. "What the hell!" He dumped his wet boot with a splash on the floor. Then the other foot-soak joined the first. "Goddamn it!" It was almost worth the rage to ruin his cheer. I knew I was in trouble, but I was glad to dampen his day. For his part, Ted didn't even wake up to hear. That morning the chores were done in silence. My father would tell this story to his friends for years to come with laughter in his voice. He'd been a bit of a prankster in his own youth. And he seemed to come to understand the jest of a Coca-cola in his Kodiak work boots. That morning he wasn't too light-hearted. I don't remember if he bought my breakfast or not.

◆

In the '50s and early '60s, the fair midways still had something of the carnival about them. That hold-over came from the sideshow attractions of the late nineteenth century when people would line up to buy tickets to catch a glimpse of the tragically deformed Elephant Man, John Merrick, or Sarah Bartje, the Hottentot Venus, who was briefly the toast of fashionable Paris. In my own midway adolescence, I paid good money to see the two-headed calf, the goat with six legs, an hermaphroditic hog. For the price of one dollar, I once saw the embryonic stages of human development. That display included an educational tour of nine pickled fetuses preserved in hermetically sealed jars, beginning with what looked like a slightly-blanched pollywog and culminating in a baby floating in formaldehyde and looking very much like the star child from Stanley Kubrick's futuristic film, *2001: A Space Odyssey*. I was also reminded of my mother's preserved jars of stewed apricots, most especially of those gone to mould, in which, when shaken, smut-covered fruit halves floated looking very much like the blue-white skulls of lost children.

In those days , before political correctness, we referred to these atmospheric spectacles as 'freak shows.' "Come one; come all. Step right up," the barkers cried to the throng, drawing our attention to their particular attraction.

One show I remember went by the name 'Amazonian Woman.' The posters promised that you would see a wild Amazonian woman who would transform into an ape before your very eyes. A reward of one-thousand dollars was promised to anyone who could prove a hoax. I bought my ticket and entered the seedy, grass-floored, wet-canvas-aroma wherein I found myself among a crowd of thirty other patrons facing an empty stage. The ringmaster entered and spoke to us briefly in hushed tones. He cautioned us not to agitate the excitable Amazonian woman about to make her first appearance before us. He warned us that she was timid and wild and prone to violence when provoked. Then he escorted her onto the stage. She was a dark-skinned, raven-haired beauty dressed only in a one-piece leopard-skin bathing suit. She was manacled wrist and ankle. Her metal bracelets were linked by a heavy chain to a ring in the floor located upstage left from whence she had come. Like Jacob Marley, she rattled her chains and performed a dance for our amusement. Just as promised, before our very eyes, she began to grow hair on her face, her arms and legs. She quickly achieved an atavistic metamorphosis and then ran ape-knuckled to the apron of the stage straining as her chains jerked tight. Everyone ran screaming for the exits. Everyone, that is, but I. I wanted my thousand dollar reward.

The ape who had frightened the crowd bore an uncanny resemblance to the railway luggage compartment gorilla from an old Three Stooges' short. But the cheap ape costume wasn't the problem. I had noticed that when she was an Amazonian woman, she had been wearing a leopard-skin swimsuit. After her transformation she wore no swimsuit. Even though the smoke and mirrors transformation had been slightly cheesy, and even though the simian phase of the show was mostly an obvious moth-furred, costume department gorilla suit, that wasn't the source of my quarrel. My thousand dollar proof involved the whereabouts of the vanishing leopard-skin swimsuit.

I called the geek forward after the Amazonian ape woman had shuffled perfunctorily off stage.

"What do ya want, kid?" he asked as if he were right out of big-top casting.

"I can prove the hoax," I replied rather smartly.

He just gave me a withering look and waited. I told him my 'swimsuit' theory.

"Go away, kid!" was all he said. With that he turned and walked off stage. Thus I learned a sucker's lesson. Thus I lost both one dollar and one thousand.

At London Fair, I saw Ronnie and Donnie Galyon, the Siamese Twins, conjoined at the belly facing each other. Born in 1952, they had gone on exhibit for money at the age of three. They continued to travel the circuit for thirty years. When I saw them, I was around fourteen. In that they were one year younger than I, they too would have been early teenagers. They journeyed everywhere in a long-bed truck with a picture window in the side looking in on their living room. A set of stairs led the spectators to a platform which provided an eye-level view into their private parlour. As I recall, they were lying on the floor facing the opposite direction from one another. One of them was watching a small black-and-white television set; the other boy was looking at the opposing wall. I think he might have been playing a game or doing a puzzle. I don't remember exactly. They both looked quite bored and never once glanced in our direction. I felt slightly shamed at my own curiosity, but they left a strong impression on my young mind.

I've seen them since on a television documentary on the life of Siamese twins. I've read that they were the last generation of unusual people to put themselves on display for money. I've also read a story that they quarrelled once and that one Galyon blackened his conjoined brother's eye with an angry fist-blow to the face.

One tent at the CNE had half-a-dozen or more marvels to behold. For the purchase of a single ticket, I saw the man who could stuff eight golf balls in his mouth at a time. I saw a sword swallower, a fire breather, the tallest man in the world who carried the smallest man in the palm of his hand. I saw the bearded lady who simply sat in a chair stroking her long black beard. I was reminded by her of an old Burma Shave billboard poem.

> The Bearded Lady
> tried a jar.
> She's now a famous
> movie star.
> Burma Shave.

I also saw a headless woman. Her decapitate body was lain out straight upon a narrow plank. Electrodes protruded from her ghoulish neck as if she were connected to a life support. Her fingers twitched; her toes wiggled. On the floor beside her left shoulder there was a bushel basket containing her severed head looking from a distance much like the last cabbage from the field. The eyes on the head were closed as if in sleep. The hair looked like a doll's hair or a cheap wig an elderly woman might wear. When one approached the body and bent over the basket for a closer look, the eyes blinked open and stared right up at you.

Some of these wonders performed astonishing acts. Some inspired admiration by simply sitting there or going for a brief walkabout. The gentle giant strode. The tiny man scurried. The bearded lady sat. The headless woman twitched and blinked. The golf-ball swallower stuffed his mouth with eight dimpled golf balls and simply stood there his cheeks bulging as with the affliction of a mumps sufferer. And the gurning man made cauliflower folds in his tongue or swallowed his own face with the backwards flap-kiss of his own loose lips. And all of that, I purchased, as I recall, for a mere two dollar bill.

I must say, I'm bewildered by political correctness which denies us the spectacles, while the emotional freaks entertain the talk show audience making spectacles of their ruined and stupid lives. Perhaps in future, someone might champion the dignity of the inbred losers who squabble and scream at one another on the Jerry Springer show which prides itself on having been labelled, 'the worst show in the history of television.' Reality TV. American Idol. Cops. I don't see the difference between some tone-deaf, caterwauling, pathetically untalented singer seeking fame and fortune by humiliating himself for want of being a star, and the gurning man making a serious buck folding his lip over his forehead. The dog pound barking of Jerry Springer's audience egging on some fat stranger seems far worse to me even than sad Ronnie and Donnie entertaining us by it simply being their bad luck to be connected at the belly from birth.

The women

REALIZE AS I LOOK back over the course of writing this book, that not much of it has been concerned with my mother. And yet, she was every bit as important to me in my formative years as my father. I suppose I might be forgiven for focussing mostly on my father and the life of the men on the farm, because this book has been about the land and about working on the land. My Grandmother Lee was certainly involved with the lambs brought in to the house to be fed warm, bottled milk when their own dams were either dead or dry. There is a photograph of my mother which appeared in the *Chatham Daily News* in which she is holding a lamb up to the light. However, on the Lee farm, it has been my experience that the women work at the house and the men work at the barn and in the fields. And as this is a barn book, a book of acres, not a book of kitchen and hearth and in that there isn't much of Vesta within the covers of this work, I've left the women mostly out of the mix.

I remember my sister being discouraged from visiting the barns especially during the bulling season. On one occasion, my father saw fit to shout at her and tell her to get to the house. We were standing a cow to the wall for breeding and my father thought that an inappropriate experience for an impressionable young girl. She tells me now that she experienced little of the calving, the lambing or the wiving of the beasts.

I never once saw either my sister or my mother drive a tractor. Though my sister was in the 4H calf club and the tri-county shorthorn calf club before that, and though she won many a prize with her expert showmanship and husbandry at the fairs, she wasn't at the barns much except for dreaming.

When I wrote the verse biography of my paternal grandfather, the publisher rightly noted that there wasn't much about my grandmother in that book. That was partly because I hadn't known her very well, since she'd died when I was only three. It was also because no one except my mother ever talked of her much. My mother often said, "Your grandmother was a saint." She loved her as a friend and respected her as an elder guide. My father always spoke of his mother as his best friend. To my knowledge, my grandfather never spoke of her after she was gone. In my book, *Stella's Journey*, dedicated to my grandmother, I wrote in a piece of snapshot fiction about the women at the house when the men came in from thrashing: "And they do not mind the work of women. They expect busy daughters and rapid invisible wives."

I do not pretend to completely understand the ways of the women in the house, for my work hours were spent mostly with the men at the barn. I'm amused and forced to see the truth in my elder cousin Hila's words, "It's better to be born a sheep on that farm than to be born a woman." Those damning words certainly ring true for the women who left. But in some way, the women who stayed, though thought of as trapped by many into a life of drudgery and female duty, in my opinion they are actually stronger for having stayed.

My cousin Susan speaks in entirely fond terms of our grandmother. Stella raised not only her own children, but the daughters of two of her children. Cousin Susan looks back with unalloyed love and respect for the woman who did her duty as a grandmother. Her selfless sacrifice, though seen in a certain unforgiving feminist light as weakness, can also be seen as the highest form of love. All who think of her, reflect not on the difficulty of her life with its tragedies and sacrifices, but also on the devotion to her family. She was of her generation. She is remembered entirely fondly and with pure admiration by all who knew her.

And so it is with my mother. In many ways she is the strongest and best person I have ever had the privilege of knowing. She is good-hearted, kind, loving, and pure. And she stayed.

She endured the difficulties of being a farmer's wife. She was born a farmer's daughter. She loves living in the country. Though she too has seen the world, she loves the land as her home.

One day my publisher and I met at the farm to work on an anthology I was commissioned to edit. We were driven indoors by the hum and whine of mosquitos drinking our blood at the picnic table under the maples in the yard. We left that sweaty slap and swat region of the lawn and went in to the cooler, insectless interiors of the house. We laid out our papers on the dining-room table and were busy shuffling pages and making hard choices. It was shearing time at the barn and my mother came into the room where we were occupied with our decisions and said, "You boys will have to clear the table. The men are coming in from working and I have to set out the dishes and the food for lunch." I know she didn't mean it exactly the way it sounded, but I also know that my companion had a good laugh at my expense. Writing isn't real work. Not on the farm. I look back to those days when I was at home stealing a few extra minutes during lunch break to slip up to my room and write. My father would call me to task from the base of the stairs, "Time to go back to work, Johnny." By which he meant, time to go back to the fields. I surrendered my pen for a pitchfork. I gave up my playing for toil. I was a good son. My father always told me so. Secretly, I was already lost from the land.

The tale of one picture falling...

MY FATHER DIED in Chatham Hospital at 9:30, a.m., Friday, March 19th, 2004. He was surrounded by those who loved him. My mother, my sister, two of her children, and my father's brother — my Uncle John — were there to ease his passing. His last words were, "I want one red apple." I was a thousand miles away under Caribbean heaven when I heard a voice saying, "Your father is no longer with you in the world." I heard that voice at the exact hour of his going. By cloud cross, I knew it to be true.

When my wife and I arrived home from holiday the following evening, we were greeted by the sad news at the door of our house. "Your father died yesterday," my son Sean informed me. I was not surprised to hear his words. I went to my desk, made a few necessary phone calls and wrote a poem in tribute to my father.

The Morning, My Father

the morning my father died
I was
walking the thousand miles
in his direction
under empty blue *wherein*

the sun came out like shirtstain
yellowed in the sleeve by sweatmarks
to such a sadness
coloured in the cloth by cotton azure

and it was
so tough temperaed
it soaked the earth
to a difficult green

while even the grass was straining to shade
against the loss of darkness
even I was locked in starwant
as I went
bronzing towards the sea
and sank to the chin
in south swell
as if I were rising
even the palms preferred an upturn
to the truth of whitened moonlight
even the shell hush
of bravery breaking

and I breathed to the fear fill
floating my heart
like a dozen still-breasted horses
drumming the sand and lashing the surf
in the splash line
of a far horizon.

My father was proud of his home. He once said to me, "I won't be the one to sell this farm." I know he hopes it might be kept in the family for many generations to come. "I see a day when your sons might return to the land," he said. As for my son Sean, he thinks that if he'd been born on the land as I was, he might have been a farmer. As it is, he is studying to be a police officer. My elder son, Dylan, is in Korea teaching English as a Second Language. It seems unlikely that we might honour Dad's wishes.

A few years back when my father and mother were quarrelling about the future, my father struck the arms of the parlour chair. In an angry voice he boomed, "I guess I may as well sell the farm!" With those words the aerial photograph of the home place fell from the wall in the dining room some twelve feet from where he sat. Upon investigation it was found that the nail was still fixed stiffly in the wall. The wire and frame on the photograph were sound. No one has ever been able to explain the fall of the photograph of the black barns. It simply fell as if to punctuate my father's foreboding words: "I guess I may as well sell the farm!" And the picture fell as if on cue, striking the floor like a well-framed ghost.

Language and the Land

M Y OCTOGENARIAN UNCLE recently said to me, "There's no such thing as agriculture any more." With this statement, he was strongly implying that many who work the earth have little regard for seasons yet to come and a lessening knowledge of seasons gone by. For him, that ugly neologism and portmanteau word, 'agribusiness' has supplanted the better word 'agriculture,' a word he greatly prefers. And with this, I wonder, is he correct? He certainly has the authority and experience with both language and the land to say out loud without fear of contradiction, "There is no agriculture any more." And to him, this is more than a sad state of affairs. This statement acknowledges a prophecy of future doom. With the passing away of agriculture, with its evolution into agribusiness, comes the death of the soil.

The word 'agriculture' has an ancient etymology. The latter half of the word has its root in the Greek word, 'cultura' meaning the tilling of the field as it is with the word 'cultivate'. The prefix agri refers back to the word 'acres'. Hence the word agriculture means the tilling of acres. The word 'cultivate' eventually evolved from its exclusively agrarian denotation into one which includes the cultivation of the mind and body. Hence the word 'culture' which once referred to cultivation of the earth has in modern parlance come to refer to learning and the arts. It seems quite a natural evolution to connect the cultivation of acres to the cultivation of the mind and to see a strong connection between agriculture and high culture, between the tilling of the earth and the literary arts in particular.

In western Judeo-Christian culture the first cultivator of the earth was also the first man to name the creatures of the field and become a guardian of animals. Old Testament Adam, whose name means, 'of the earth,' was given the monomastic task of naming all. His son Cain became the first husbander of animals. Adam's other son Abel tilled the earth. One of the first cultures in recorded history to achieve a sufficient surplus, achieved that abundance in the fertile crescent of the Tigris and Euphrates rivers where America now wages war on Saddam. The source of that first abundance is believed to be a grass of the wheat family called, Emma wheat. Only today, as I write this account on October 14th, 2003, the news reports on farmers' resistance to genetically-altered wheat reveal a knowledge of the possible impact of science upon future generations. What began as an observation of a plant capable of producing sufficient yields to support an urban population in the Middle East, has led eventually to a generation of genetically-altered wheat which is 'Round-Up-Ready', weed resistant, and capable of supporting huge yields with a minimum of further human intervention. At the same time, there are other issues at hand which farmers see as relevant and imperative to the far-sighted men who see into the future and fear the tyranny of the present and a slavish adherence to the notions of a tight connection between change and progress as inevitably synonymous with improvement.

A favourite quotation of my father's comes to mind. He likes to say, "the art of progress is the preservation of order in the midst of change, and the preservation of change in the midst of order." He is a farmer quoting a philosopher. I am a poet, quoting a farmer. Everything I know about literature, I learned on the farm. My father's name is George. My sister's name is Georgina. George means 'farmer.' Georgina means, 'farmer's daughter.'

The word farmer derives its meaning from the fifteenth century Latin word 'firma.' The 'firma' was the rental paid by a tenant who worked the land. This word evolved into the words farm and farmer. The firma was the rent paid, the farm was the acreage of rental, and the farmer was originally the one who collected the rent. By the fifteenth century, the farmer became the man who worked the land.

Why does it matter what words mean? How does the knowledge of such meaning have impact upon the way we see the land? To some it may not matter that the word 'civilized' originally meant 'city dweller,' and that as a corollary the word 'civilization,' at its simplest level means 'city.' Yet history teaches us that cities exist only as a result of surplus and such abundance is directly related to the assured and continued success of agriculture. Civilization depends upon the availability of food. Culture comes from cultivation. Culture depends upon leisure and abundance. The great achievements of civilization are entirely rooted in the success of agriculture. Without abundance, there is no permanent settlement. Without permanent settlement, there is no accumulation of recorded knowledge. Literacy, the invention of written language, depends upon leisure. Leisure and the luxury of formal learning depend upon abundance. Abundance depends upon a reliable and permanently available food source. Literature is deeply and ineluctably rooted in the humus of cultivated grasses. Poetry is the fruit of wheat.

If, as I believe and have stated in the past, "Everything comes from the earth, even the sky begins on the ground," then we are talking of important matters. Poetry which is not somehow rooted in the land, blows away. I recently read that we humans see the stars twinkling because of the effect of the earth's atmosphere.

Despite our heliocentric planetary system, our entire experience is geocentric. Life depends not only upon water, but also upon fertile ground. Food is not born in the grocery store. The hamburger in the fast food outlet is not created from nothing in a back room and built on the grill by a clown in big red wig. I fear for those who lose sight of the original. High-rise living is often so much of a simulacrum. A shadow of life without origin. We pave paradise at our peril. And yet, it seems we live within the influence of dramatic extremes.

The long history of the relationship between human beings and arable land has led to two perilous poles of thought. Both are equally destructive. Both have their mad champions. At the one extreme stands the idea of absolute ownership. Private enterprise at worst gives rise to the opportunity for the temporary accumulation of individual wealth. A person who accepts this philosophy might be heard to say, "It's my land. I'll do with it whatever I want."

Thus we might: Poison the wells. Mine the gravel. Level the forest. Steal the streams. Drain the swamps. Starve the rivers. Deplete the earth and leave behind a ruin. A desert. A waterless place. Chernobyl and the thousand year desolation. Dust bowls. Death valleys. Salt flats. Leached earth economics leading to a weary waste. We might all thus become, to paraphrase the words of T.S. Eliot, "old men in a dry season."

The other extreme encourages a return of cultivated land to the wilderness and the wilds. We suffer nostalgia for the peaceable kingdom. We long to go back to the garden. We yearn to restore a pre-human paradise where man has no permanent place. At its worst, this view sees humanity as existing outside of nature. Not as an Adamic guardian, but as a parasite and great destroyer. This leads to a romancing of weeds. We are portrayed as a supra-natural pestilence. At its most ridiculous, this philosophy is based upon a complete denial of the reality of our predicament. We might be portrayed as the only pathetic creatures capable of hearing how even the vegetables scream. The wolf has no such crisis of the conscience of the carnivore. Nor does the cow suffer for her silage. What might we do? As worms—eat dirt? As oaks—eat air?

Nature might provide for the lazy hermit, but not for the lethargic crowd. Our population depends upon surplus for its survival. Whether we like it or not, the future of humanity depends upon cultivation and agriculture. It requires that we acknowledge and honour our predicament and our place in nature.

Permanent fallowing and failure to cultivate arable land leads to more than noble monkish ascetisicm. It leads to the lunatic fringe. The Unibomber as an example of one man living off the land. The man who believed so devoutly in the parables of the Old Testament that he raised a tiger and a gator in his Manhattan apartment believing that he was re-establishing the peaceable kingdom. Thus we become the food of beasts. The literalist eventually becomes someone's supper. This is a strong argument for both realism and for an understanding of both the power of the land and the power of the written word as metaphor and as allegory.

Both waste and wilderness lead to starvation. Of these two extremes, the former seems to me by far the worse. A return to the wilderness may lead to the starvation of the few who go that way. This is a foolish hunger. Even whole-earth hippies eventually come back to the city for hamburgers and fries, a dry warm place to sleep and a hot bath to wash the land from their hands. This other, this 'business-driven' paradigm seems bound to lay waste the weary earth. In California, salination. In Florida, sinkholes. In the North American west, dust and wind. In South America, the destruction of the rainforest sometimes referred to as the lungs of the earth. In the world, warming of the ice cap, disappearance of the ozone, and the signs are everywhere that we are on the verge of changes beyond our control.

Fortunately for all, most of us have until quite recently occupied the middle ground. Our past, though only mostly rooted in a relatively recent scientific revolution of the late 18th century, has been for the most part either benign or beneficial to the earth. Even if we have a sense of the distant past, still by the principles of scientific farming beginning with the likes of Jethro Tull in England and Thomas Jefferson in America, we have a sense that we follow in the path of great ideas and that we are part of a continuum in which ideas of progress and ideas of improvement are synonymous. In this, we have a sense of ourselves as on the path of the good.

I was born and raised into that tradition. I made a moral from my grandfather's words, "A farmer should leave the land in better condition when he is done with it, than it was in when he began working it. The land is more than the grave of the father. It is also the soil of the son." And so, I saw in his past, my father's present task. The one I refused when I departed for the bookish life. The life of learning. The life of the poet. And because I became a poet, I paid close attention to the literature that was there for me in the hall bookshelf at home on the farm.

I listened to my uncle who quoted from Virgil's *Georgics* at the fair barns. The *Georgics* is a two-thousand year old text containing most everything the Romans knew on farming. The court poet, Virgil, was a farmer's son. I listened when my grandfather quoted Shakespeare's shepherds, and when he acknowledged Biblical husbandry predating Mendel and that monk's quite recent genetic interference with peas. I read Canada's first modern poet, Raymond

Knister, whose father raised purebred workhorses and was a fruit farmer living on land near Cedar Springs, only a few kilometers from where I grew up. I read Lampman, a minister's son from Morpeth, who wrote about haying. Though a village lad, he worked on the surrounding farms as a boy. I followed with a certainty in my grandfather's grandfather's footsteps. I was born to the same ground under the same blue sky as the man who almost two-hundred years ago left Ireland for a better life in Canada.

When, I recently discovered and read the work of Romantic era poet, John Clare, I came to recognize the destructive possibilities in the idea of progress. Clare was born in England on the cusp of the closures. He was born a ploughman's son in the era of a great revolution in farming. He loved the meandering streams, the undrained swales, the crooked roads which curved to avoid disturbing the ancient English oak. He worked while the sun shone and took his rest in doomed shade. He wrote about loss. Scientific farming dug straight ditches, built straight roads, drained swamps, felled the great trees, destroyed ancient ecologies, and provided food for England while Europe starved. It has been argued by one historian that crop variety and the agricultural revolution which ended the less aggressive cultivation of the land romanticized as paradise by Clare, made it possible for England to feed its people while France starved. France's resistance to change, and its over-reliance upon wheat and bread led to starvation of urban populations and thereby to inevitable violent revolution.

Hard not to see Clare's romantic view as idyllic. The image of the poet dreaming in the shade, is an attractive cliche difficult to resist. Just as the pastoral and lazy heat of Lampman leads one to wish for a hot day in the hay, so too, Clare's frog swamps and ancient oaks seduce us into believing his to have been a better world. And yet, I've worked in the hay and found the drudgery and soul death in labour there. And I've witnessed the lovely results of well over a hundred years of husbandry.

Somewhere between what's best for business and what's best for the soil lies the better path. Somewhere between super peccaries with their poisonous lagoons and the ecoli-contaminated wells, and the lovely complexity of an unspoiled wilderness lies the best future for us all.

In that literature is neither an argument nor a persuasion, we might well ask and require a satisfactory answer to the question, "What is the purpose to be found in the work of the poet who writes of rural things?" If, as I believe, the role of literature is to accurately imagine the past, to pay astute and reliable attention to the present, and to be ever-mindful of a well-remembered future, then this it shares with the best examples in the history and traditions of agriculture. Literature does not instruct us in a way to behave, though it may record both the best and the worst in our behaviours and the consequences of our choices. It also might provide a record and a deep accounting of human experience worthy of attention and the beauty of expression. Art rooted in reality also transforms reality. Literature, if not instructing us on a path to take, at least illuminates the possibilities of each chosen path. The redactor of the Pentateuch. Virgil. The translators of the Bible. Piers the Ploughman. John Clare. Archibald Lampman. Raymond Knister. Robert Frost. Wendell Berry. These we follow. Thus we lead.

> *Far Spread the moory ground, a level scene*
> *Bespread with rush and one eternal green*
> *That never felt the rage of blundering plough*
> *Though centuries wreathed spring's blossoms on its brow...*

from *"The Moors"*, by John Clare

What Will We Do if the Rhino Dies?

*A*T *AGE EIGHTEEN I left the farm on the hill I called home. For all my thought, my shade had made such a small improvement on the ground, my shadow grew to leave the lane. Though there was but a little of Lampman in me, and even less of Clare, I'd set out not to be a farmer, but to become a poet on my own.*

Though I've never needed sleep to dream, I had a sleeping dream. My father and I had spent the light walking the fields about the barns and so had measured from four directions what he owned. That night in bed at home, I'd seen a fence my father'd built to keep the rhino in.

"What will we do if the rhino dies?" my father had asked upon finding the dream-gate wide with the rhino gone.

Being the prodigal, I did not need a Joseph to tell me what the rhino was. I'd gone away and nothing but my voice returned.